Tales From The Parks
My Adventures as a Park Ranger

Russell Cahill

TALES FROM THE PARKS
By Russell Cahill
© 2016 Russell Cahill

Cover design by Gwen Gades
Edited by Elizabeth MS Flynn
Print ISBN: 978-1534636460
           1534636463

http://www.russellcahill.com

"A man who loves the world beyond his understanding, welcoming its unexpected blessings and depending on them, in spite of its unexpected trials and dangers, has the wisdom of a man long married to a beloved woman."

— From *The Unforeseen Wilderness: An Essay on Kentucky's Red River Gorge* by Wendell Berry

For Susie Menger Cahill 1938–1982

INTRODUCTION

For three generations before me, the Cahill men have been seamen. My Irish great-grandfather worked his way to Hawai'i on a ship, married a Hawai'ian woman and stayed. He was there when the kingdom was taken over by American merchants. My grandfather studied mechanics at Lahainaluna School and became a marine engineer. Both of my grandfathers served on ships during the First World War and my grandfather Cahill, who survived two sinkings in World War II, was joined at sea by my father and one of his brothers. The rest of the family built and repaired ships and my aunt Hessie worked for the US Navy for fifty years. My seagoing father wanted me to study engineering. But the ship's bell did not call me to sea; I wanted to be a park ranger.

Join me on a journey across this great land we know as the United States. Travel with me from the grandeur of the Yosemite, through the far reaches of Alaska, east to the White House, and west to the middle of the Pacific Ocean. Along the way, around the campfire, I will tell you of the adventures of a park ranger in the 1960s and 1970s and the people and creatures I met along the way. I hope you will enjoy the journey as much as I did.

CHAPTER 1

Big Basin State Park — 1948

I believe if you set me down blindfolded in California's Big Basin State Park, I would know where I had landed by the smell of the redwood forest, the sounds of the wind high in those magnificent sequoias and the raucous calls of Steller's jays and acorn woodpeckers. I would be standing in a carpet of redwood sorrel alongside a tree with the thick bark colored an unforgettable shade of red-brown. There is a memorial grove in the Basin dedicated to my late wife Susie and my mother's ashes are scattered in the place she loved. If we, in this life, are given a home place, Big Basin is mine.

I was born in San Francisco, a *hapa haole* (half white) child of a mother who traced her ancestry to the Pilgrims and a Hawai'ian father who traced his to the coming of Polynesian voyagers to Hawai'i somewhere around 600 AD. My four sisters and my brother were also born in the Bay Area and we carried on a tradition from my mother's family, camping in Big Basin every summer.

The park is situated in the Santa Cruz Mountains sixty-four miles south of San Francisco. Its origin is a classic story of people banding together to make something good happen. In 1899, *Wide World Magazine*, an English publication, hired a San Jose photographer and painter named Andrew P. Hill to take pictures of the redwood trees. Hill traveled to Felton, California, and began photographing trees in a grove that is now Henry Cowell Redwoods State Park. He was kicked out of the forest by the landowner. Infuriated, Hill began a movement to save the redwood forest for public enjoyment.

Hill and his friends found better groves at Big Basin, enlisted leading Californians, and organized a group called the Sempervirens Club, named for the coast redwood's scientific name, *Sequoia sempervirens.* They lobbied the legislature, which appropriated $250,000, an amount equivalent to more than $7 million in today's currency. Private sources raised matching funds, and the first unit of the California State Park System was founded. The original park consisted of 3,200 acres. Over the years, using the matching funds raised in the private sector, the park has been expanded to 18,000 acres and covers land from the summit of the mountains all the way to the sea.

There are photographs of my mother, Dorothy Hutchinson, at age six posing next to an old flat-bed truck, camping with her extended family. She caused a stir when she and a twelve-year-old companion were lost for two days when they wandered away from the camp. The missing girls were front-page news in

California. A huge search ensued and the two wayfarers were finally located at the Hoover family ranch. They had walked twelve miles along Wadell Creek, eating berries as they made their way to the coast following the deer trails alongside the creek.

My sisters and I loved the camping trips. We picked huckleberries that my mother seemed to magically convert into a delicious confection called huckleberry buckle on top of the wood-burning camp stove. We dangled pieces of bologna from strings and caught crawdads. Led by my intrepid older sister Anona, we hung out in a shallow limestone cave, prepared to hold off all enemies. There was a roughed-out concrete swimming area fed by a creek where we learned to swim. And the park had a pavilion hung with Japanese lanterns where, on warm evenings, rangers played records and dances were held where kids had their first experience dancing two-steps under the watchful eyes of a park ranger.

The park was very different than it is today. While giving nature walks, long hikes and evening campfire talks, the rangers also provided other entertainment. I recall listening to the Joe Louis–Jersey Joe Wolcott rematch on a portable radio that rangers set up at the campfire circle. At night we'd all walk to the campfire, sing songs, and hear a short talk from a ranger before walking back with our flashlights and snuggling into sleeping bags for the night.

Each morning, I would show up for the nature walk or longer hike. I'd listen and try to memorize the ranger talk. Harriet "Petey" Weaver, the first woman California State Park Ranger, was the best. She was a tall woman with a strong voice and she had infinite patience with ten-year-olds. She taught me about the remarkable survival abilities of the great trees and showed me salamanders and rubber boas. Back at our camp I would recount the journey to my mother, who also had great amounts of patience. Sometimes I talked Mom into going with me on the shorter hikes where I would, to the best of my ability, repeat what Ranger Weaver had told me.

Together with many other families in the post–World War II era, we branched out to other parks. We climbed around a Cascade mountain at Lassen Volcano National Park, where we saw and smelled our first evidence of a volcano that was just dozing and not dead. We camped among marauding bears at Yellowstone, where we saw our first wild bears and we spent a week or so in Yosemite Valley, a place that would later become my home. We towed a homemade cargo trailer loaded with surplus army tents, a Coleman stove, and an ice chest. A flax water bag hung from the back of the car where our drinking water was cooled by evaporation. I chronicled our travels on a camera I had earned selling subscriptions on my paper route. At age twelve I fell in love with some girl at nearly every park. Generally, the romance lasted less than 48 hours.

Sometime around 1950 I started understanding conservation. It was probably during a trip to Calaveras Big-Trees State Park. It is a short way down the hill from Angel's Camp, the place of Mark Twain's jumping frog story. There, we found some huge giant sequoia trees. They are the more massive cousins of the coast redwoods found in coastal California and are the biggest and some of the oldest living things. A signature attraction in the park is a stump that is more than 25 feet in diameter. In 1853, in an act of unbelievable vandalism, the tree was cut down by tourism entrepreneurs. Its bark was removed and a large section was displayed at World's Fairs here and in England.

A story told around the campfire was that dozens of curious people had ridden in on horseback and in carriages from Sacramento and the Bay Area to witness the cutting. According to the story teller, after the sawyers finished the cuts, the tree could not be coaxed over with wedges or other methods, so everyone went off to their lodgings for the night. During the night, the wind gave it a nudge and it fell without witnesses. Many people believed Mother Nature disapproved of having an audience witness this desecration. When I saw the stump, it had served as a post office, and later a dance pavilion since the tree's falling. When I got home, I joined the Save the Redwoods League as a junior member and became involved in conservation projects with the Boy Scouts.

An article in the *Guardian*, written by Leo Hickman on June 27, 2013, postulated that the outrage over the cutting of the Calaveras "Discovery Tree" in 1853 started a movement that resulted in President Abraham Lincoln and the US Congress in 1865 setting Yosemite and the Mariposa Grove aside in a protective status. It certainly had a role in the beginning of the drive for state and national parks.

Dreaming of Wild Places

During World War II we lived in a red brick house in Edgemar, the first village south of San Francisco along the coast highway. The town was occupied by a couple of dozen Bohemians and a few early commuters who braved the dangerous cliffside road every day. The coastal communities of Sharp Park, Vallemar, and Rockaway, never more than a thousand or so in population, are now called Pacifica and are home to 35,000 or so and growing.

During my childhood, I had the run of the coastal sand dunes, cliffs and beaches. Together with my sisters Anona, Lani, and Jane, I picked wild strawberries and roamed the hills without worrying about any danger other than that of nature. I saw gray whales, seals, and sea lions along the coast and found all kinds of creatures of the sea washed ashore. There were no signs warning of big waves or anything else, but I mostly kept in mind my mother's warnings and her tolerance for rambunctious children.

My uncle Fred came home during the war with burns on a lot of his body and a Bronze Star for bravery. He had been lowered with fire control equipment into a burning gap in the side of the aircraft carrier *Saratoga* after it had been hit by a kamikaze aircraft. My father was still at sea and Fred spent a lot of time with me while his burns healed. He made a surf fishing pole from an eleven-foot piece of bamboo, bought me a Montgomery Ward surf reel, and spent time teaching me to fish in the surf along San Francisco's beaches. There is also no better place to become interested in nature than along those beaches. Whales passed by, live-bearing perch spilled their offspring in the surf, and I dug invertebrates from the sand for bait. I caught my first salmon near the Farallon Islands on a trip with Fred and my cousin Gigi from a boat that would never pass Coast Guard inspection today.

A few years after my father returned from the war, he taught me to hunt. Most of my friends had .22 rifles or BB guns and were shooting the hell out of birds, electric pole insulators, and other targets. I was not allowed to have one. When I was eleven, my father bought two World War I Springfield 30.06 rifles and had the weapons adapted for hunting. My first efforts at the rifle range caused some bruising on my shoulder, but the message got through: this weapon is not a toy.

Dad taught me gun safety, marksmanship, and respect for what the rifle could do. We hunted deer in the mountains of Mendocino County, in the front range of the Lassen Country and in the wild lands of Modoc County on California's northeast corner. I remember seeing big herds of pronghorns on the dry lakes on the Nevada border and watching a golden eagle soar above the cliffs. I killed my first deer at age twelve and learned from my father to respect the animals we hunted for our food.

Like many of the boys in my community, the Boy Scouts were a big part of my life. Returning veterans taught me to cook outdoors, track animals, and survive in the wilderness. One wounded vet, a one-armed Scout master in Sharp Park named Bob Pope, taught us to box with his very effective left jab. At age fifteen I spent ten days in a wilderness south of Sonora Pass with twenty or so other boys mapping a place called Lewis Lakes that had been located incorrectly on some maps.

During my teen years, my friends and I backpacked in the Sierra Nevada Mountains and in the Los Padres National Forest. We had no fancy equipment, making do with coffee cans converted into twig-burning stoves, and some military surplus packs and sleeping bags. We hiked in canvas shoes and would have been astonished had we hit a time warp and walked into an REI or Cabela's and seen the variety of goods and the high prices we take for granted today. The net result of all this outdoor recreation was a growing desire to bend my life in the direction of the wilds.

CHAPTER 2

Coming of Age in the 1950s

Campbell Union High School was one of those places we see in all the California-stereotype movies set in the 1950s. The girls wore full skirts and short-sleeved sweaters and carried thirty pounds of books tightly held against their chests. Most of the boys wore "peggers," with pants tailored so the bottoms were tight below the knees. Gangster boys had "duck's-ass" haircuts and many of my friends had flat-top haircuts. My school had a significant population of Japanese-American kids who were not long out of the internment camps and lots of second-generation Mexican-Americans. During the 1950s, there was an innocence that seems to have been lost since then. There were plenty of bad things going on. We knew of students who used heroin, and we knew about abuse and sexual assault. But without television and the Internet, they just didn't seem to be constantly in one's face.

Campbell was an excellent school, with fine teachers and plenty of encouragement for people who wanted to go to college. I got good grades and was the league's leading scorer in football and a gold medalist in track and field. I sang in the choir and was elected to student council. Instead of the hot rods driven in the movies, I had a 1940 Chevy that cost $50 and was without a reverse gear. It got me to jobs on the weekends and over the hill to the beach for body surfing. I fell in love with Susie Menger, a lovely girl with a talent for painting and an ability to deflate my ego whenever it exceeded her limits of tolerance. Susie came from a family of Michigan farmers and was a delight to be with. We were together for twenty-seven years until she was taken by leukemia.

I was recruited by half a dozen or so universities. I selected Southern Methodist University and had a lot of encouraging correspondence from them until they asked for a photograph. I sent one taken when I was on the track team, and between my Hawai'ian DNA and a lot of sun exposure, I was pretty dark. The following week I received a one-sentence rejection letter. At the time, the color barricades were up in Texas and every place east of Texas. Football, coupled with good grades, got me an athletic scholarship to Michigan State University. I was driven to East Lansing by my family. My father gave me $100 and a good luck hug and I've been on my own ever since. I registered as an engineering student, but a flunking grade in analytic geometry and calculus caused me to reconsider. After making up the class, I stuck to required courses until I figured out what I wanted to do with my life.

During the summer of 1957, Susie and I married in Campbell and headed back to Lansing, where she had grown up. She had studied for a secretarial certificate at Heald's Business College in San Jose and was hired by the university. I played in early-season MSU football games as a varsity backup center and linebacker but only in the event we were leading by thirty points. The starting player was Dan Curry, an All-American and future NFL player. He had a couple of years of eligibility left and I had been converted from fullback. I wasn't much of a center although the ability to create chaos as a linebacker was enjoyable, but eventually my scholarship was taken away and given to some more promising incoming player. Tuition costs for out-of-state students were prohibitive, so Susie and I decided to go home to California. We loaded up the old Ford woody and headed west at the end of the quarter. I had learned some good things at Michigan State and gotten a head start on college and had no regrets about the experience.

The draft was hanging over my head, so I enlisted in the Army Reserve and went off to Fort Ord for six months of training. Basic training was followed by truck driving school and a few weeks driving a "six by six" around Monterey County.

On one beautiful sunny day, I got a weekend pass from Fort Ord, drove to San Jose, picked up Susie and headed to Big Basin State Park for a day hike. On the way down the twisty two-lane Highway 9, I came around a corner and found a car partially blocking the road. A family's car had quit at a bad spot, so Susie hiked back around the corner to flag down any other cars, and I helped the driver push the car to a wider spot. We were several miles from a telephone, so Susie stayed with the woman and the children, who were nervous about being stuck there, and I drove the husband down the twisty road to park headquarters to call for a tow truck.

On the way back to the disabled car, the man asked me what I did for a living and I told him I was getting out of the Army in about a month. When I got him back to his car, he handed me his business card and said, "Call the number on the back of this card when you get out and I'll help you get a job." I thanked him and picked up Susie and headed back down the road.

At the park I looked at the card. The man's name was L. Eugene Root and he was vice president in charge of the enormous Lockheed Missile System operation in Sunnyvale and in Southern California. Good luck or karma, call it what you will, but upon discharge from active duty, I went to work as an engineering assistant building Polaris submarine–launched guided missiles.

The military–industrial complex paid for the rent and the groceries for a year. I got a raise to two bucks an hour and thought I was on the way up. But someone else was on the way. Susie was pregnant and I needed a better job. At the end of my year at Lockheed, I took the exam for deputy sheriff in Santa Clara County. I scored well, passed the physical exam and the fitness tests, and became a deputy sheriff in 1959, a couple of months before the birth of Tim, our first child.

Note:

The sheriff's department exam was a half-day written test taken by three hundred or so of us hoping to get hired in one of the seven openings. Using all the testing techniques I'd learned in college, I stayed until the end and was the last to turn in my answers. A sergeant named Moe Gilleran was collecting the tests. Some went into one pile, but others had the face page torn off and the test answers tossed into a garbage can. Mine went into the main pile and I asked him what was happening. Sgt. Gilleran told me that if you couldn't spell "deputy sheriff" on the face page where you printed your name and the position you were being tested for, they didn't bother to score the rest and you'd get a failure postcard notice. Fortunately, I didn't flunk the two-word spelling test.

Pinning on the First Badge

Back then, there was no preliminary training, no police academy. Our training consisted of working two to a car night beats with an experienced officer. We were issued a badge, handcuffs, and an allowance to buy our first uniform. The pistol, holster, and leathers were all purchased on our own nickel. I was assigned to ride midnight shift with a deputy named Don Linscott, and to this day, I thank my stars. Don taught me what I needed to know to keep myself safe and to back him up. I studied the state laws and local ordinances and between midnight and eight a.m., Don would quiz me and tutor me on how to do the job. The sheriff's department had been undergoing a change from the bad old days and had a number of people on the force who had gotten four-year degrees at San Jose State College's police administration program. Don was one of those, and I learned my craft from an ethical and very competent deputy.

Life lessons are there for the asking when you work the streets on the night shift. I was a young "hot dog" talking trash about the people we dealt with. A sergeant pulled me aside one night and brought me up short. "Look, your job isn't to reform these people, it's to herd them," he told me. "Someone else will do the reforming. Just get out there and try to keep them from hurting themselves and others." He quietly pointed out some officers who had serious problems and told me, "There are two roads in this job. On one you will get out there and help people to be better and you will be better for it. The other road has you assuming everyone is crap. You'll get an ulcer, an alcohol problem, and die from a heart attack the day after you retire." The advice was simple, easy to remember, and it stuck with me for the rest of my life.

The years of the early 1960s were times of change. We guarded the Beatles at their hotel in Palo Alto, and Nikita Khrushchev when he visited the IBM plant. I was assigned to guard the starting line at the first US versus Russia track meet that was held at Stanford University. There were riots in Watts, President John F. Kennedy was assassinated, and federal troops were being sent south to help integrate schools. Hallucinogens were readily available and in common use. The scourge of heroin was on the rise and tense international differences with Soviet bloc nations were causing personal fear and distress on the part of the people we were there to protect.

It was about this time I also started to understand the racial divide in law enforcement. Our county was transitioning from an agricultural economy to manufacturing. It had a substantial population of Mexican-Americans, both citizens and visiting agricultural workers. There was also a community of African-Americans and a big Asian population. But of the three hundred or so deputies there was one Mexican-American, one Asian, and me, a half-Hawai'ian. There were no black employees at all. Racial jokes and poor treatment of minorities was a tradition and as far as the jokes went, I was as guilty as the next guy. But I was in the vanguard as change began and I started to detect the pattern.

Among the deputies, I was an expert shot with the pistol. Our required firing range sessions were very competitive, and on one day I shot a perfect score on the practical police course, a mobile session during which we ran between barricades and fired from different positions and distances, sometimes using our "off" hand. Our captain was also a fine shot and usually won the competition. When the results, a tie, were announced by the range master, the captain said, "When did you Abos stop throwing rocks?"

A nasty answer on the tip of my tongue stayed there, and I did the next best thing. I picked up a fist-sized rock and heaved it 85 feet toward the silhouette target. Now here's the thing. If you asked me to try that, I'd undoubtedly overthink it and miss. But anger and some unknown ability caused that rock to fly right through the ten-point area on the target. I didn't have to insult the captain, and my cohorts loved it. (In my novel *Kolea*, Hawai'ian warriors throw a lot of rocks. Perhaps it's an inherited ability.) The incident caused me to start seeing the absurdity and cruelty of making fun of the nonwhites we dealt with and I stopped telling or laughing at the racial jokes.

On a weekly basis and during two-week summer training sessions, I attended drills at the US Army Reserve 306th Military Police Company in San Jose. I fulfilled my service obligation over the next six years, and became a platoon sergeant and the principal instructor for all handheld weapons. The training helped me with my job, and I came to know many other law enforcement people who were in the same reserve unit.

Night shifts allowed me to get back to my education, and I enrolled at San Jose State College in the law enforcement administration program. But in the back of my mind, the seed planted long ago in Big Basin started to grow. I lived next door to some students who were seasonal park rangers at Crater Lake National Park and Pinnacles National Monument. During vacations, Susie and I would throw the kids and camping gear in the car and visit these fellows at their parks where we got an insider's look at the National Park Service. I drove to the Park Service office in San Francisco and asked what was necessary for me to become a park ranger. The answer was that I should leave the police administration program I was enrolled in and major in a natural science. In the following quarter I became a biology major with a specialty in entomology.

During one semester I turned in for grading the best collection of night flying insects anyone had seen. I was assigned night duty patrolling the south part of the county in places where radio communications were bad to nonexistent. The radio operators would call on their powerful transmitter, and I would drive to the nearest phone booth and call in. The circular fluorescent lights in those booths attracted lots of insects, and I carried a cyanide collecting jar under the seat of the patrol car and when calling in, I'd scoop the doomed hexapods into the jar and take them home for curating. It was the 1960s and I had no desire to turn in fellow students for possessing a marijuana joint or other widespread college student offenses, so I didn't advertise my occupation as a law enforcement officer. Many other students believed I was just a zealot spending my nights out hunting insects.

The other requirement for a ranger position was getting a passing grade on the Federal Service Entrance Examination. For three years prior to graduating, I took the exam for practice. I also acquired a practice exam book and spent odd hours learning how the test was structured and answering practice questions. Some of my required classes could not be done part time, so in 1965 I resigned from the sheriff's department and took full-time class loads.

We had three children by then, and Susie took a job working nights at Western Electric in Sunnyvale while I juggled my classes and worked weekends as a bouncer at a go-go club and worked occasional relief midnight shifts at Langendorf and Sunlite Bakeries. On occasion, I would get short assignments from the sheriff's department and once served as a bailiff at a sensational murder trial. Neither Susie nor I got much sleep that year, but I graduated in June of 1966.

When I finally took the exam for real, the practice paid off. My score was so high, I was getting calls from three federal agencies within a week of taking the test. Offers came for investigator positions with the Customs Service, the Navy, and the Civil Service Commission. My real goal was the National Park Service, and during the following week I got the call I had been waiting for. A man named John Mahony was the regional forester for the Western Region of National Parks. He interviewed me in his office in downtown San Francisco. His first statement to me was, "This biology degree is just fine, but what we're really interested in is your law enforcement experience." So times were changing.

Murphy's Law: And I Improve My Chess and Spanish

My parks career started out at the Tri-Valley Grower's cannery out on Thirteenth Street in San Jose. I was supposed to enter ranger training in June but due to a bureaucratic snafu, someone lost my paperwork and I had to wait until September. So I spent the summer at the end of the juice line lifting 32-ounce cans of fruit juice off the end of a conveyor belt with a device that allowed me to catch seven of them at a time and then stack them onto a palette. All summer I dreamed of being a park ranger.

My work partner at the cannery was a CPA from Mexico with a work permit. He made more money lifting cans in San Jose than he could make auditing books in Mexico, and he sent most of it home. His English was almost nonexistent and my Spanish was poor. We worked on our language skills together. Each of us would load one palette while the other rested and then we'd switch.

My partner turned out to be an excellent chess player. He told me he had been employed by a timber company in Mexico. He kept the books at a remote lumber camp during the week and rode the log train home on the weekends. The people at the camp would get together after work and set up a chessboard. Those in the railroad station at the other end of the line would set up a similar board. Each move was argued over by the group. Then they would send the agreed move by telegraph to the other end. At the end of the week, the losers bought beer after the train brought the loggers home. I had a small peg-board chess set. I brought it to the cannery and each of us made one move every time we switched tasks. I never won a game, but by the time I left for the Park Service in September, my chess game, my Spanish, and my biceps were all greatly improved.

CHAPTER 3

Becoming a Ranger — 1966

Susie and I loaded up the car with Tim, Joan, Matt, and our belongings, said our good-byes and drove off to Arizona. The Horace M. Albright Training Center is perched on the South Rim of the Grand Canyon. At nearly 7,000-feet elevation it takes a little getting used to if you are a sea-level person. The rim of the canyon is just a short walk from the academy, and it is peppered with names like Grand View. It overlooks one of the most spectacular vistas on the planet. The school was an eleven-week basic training academy for park rangers. My family was issued a nice furnished apartment and my oldest child, Tim, enrolled in school. A store in the canyon village had basics, but a 75-mile drive to Flagstaff every couple of weeks was necessary for groceries and other needs.

During the 1960s, many park rangers who had joined the National Park Service after serving in World War II were retiring. These rangers had been on the job during the growth years when Americans and their visitors flocked to the parks to sightsee and camp in these remarkable places. The retirements and the need for replacements meant great opportunities for those of us who were lucky to enter the service in the mid-1960s.

My fellow rangers came from all over. One was a former hay farmer from Minnesota. Another had been a lieutenant commander in the Navy. There were park superintendents from Australia and Thailand sent for training. The three women in the class were classified as park ranger-historians because the NPS had not yet allowed women into the regular park ranger ranks. The women performed all of the training with the rest of us. With the exceptions of the part of my heritage that is Hawai'ian, and Boon Saisorn, the manager of the Khao Yai National Park in Thailand, every member of the NPS class was white. There was a tiny scattering of Native Americans, Latinos, and Asian-Americans serving in the Park Service in 1966, but among the Permanent Ranger Corps I knew of no African-Americans except for one guy in the Virgin Islands. Although there had been two national parks in Hawai'i since the formation of the service in 1916, I believe I was the first park ranger of native Hawai'ian ancestry.

I met Cleve and Marty Pinnix at training. They were newlyweds and had made the trip west from North Carolina driving a VW Squareback loaded with their belongings. Cleve was later to become the director of the Washington State Parks and we have been close friends ever since we left the training center. When the uniform suppliers showed up to fit us with our World War I–style uniforms, the size difference between us amused us, with Cleve, a thin fellow, having the narrowest of the coats, while mine, one of the widest. Everyone was fitted for the Stetson "flat hat," except for the women, who were fitted with what looked like 1949 airline attendant outfits with little fabric hats designed after the ones worn on Pan American World Airlines. During the following decade, the service began to integrate and women battled their way through a series of ridiculous uniform selections until they finally got to wear the same wonderfully archaic uniforms worn by the rest of us. The hats, similar to those worn by Canadian Mounties, have a very strong and stiff brim. On my first day in uniform, I was wearing the Stetson when I bent to kiss Susie good-bye and nearly broke her nose.

The training of park rangers was the most comprehensive and varied thing going at the time. We qualified with pistols on one day and learned to fill out dozens of bureaucratic forms on the next. We learned mountain rescue while dangling over the side of Grand Canyon cliffs gripping a Stokes litter containing a terrified fellow trainee and followed that with lessons on giving nature walks and speaking to crowds of hundreds at evening campfire programs. We disassembled movie projectors in the morning, packed horses and mules in the afternoon, and ran compass courses in the night. The FBI taught us the rules of evidence and how to disarm someone pointing a pistol at us. We learned how to do health and safety inspections at restaurants in order to protect visitors from salmonella and other ailments and how to apply a traction splint to a skier with a compound fractured femur.

There was never a more eclectic and comprehensive course of study. Today, the service has given in to specialization, so the generalist-ranger is no more. With, admittedly, the perspective of someone on the downside of his seventies, I am glad for the chance I was given to experience that transitory time. Things were simple. When you got to your park, you did *everything*. And it turned out that during the next four decades I used darned near everything I had been taught at the Albright Training Center.

Assignment Day

After successfully completing ten-plus weeks of training, we finally arrived at the terror of assignment day at the Albright Training Center. Would you be assigned to Federal Hall on Wall Street in New York City or find yourself riding with a pack string at Yellowstone? Would you freeze your ass off at Katmai in Alaska or be assigned to the "Cannonball Circuit" of Civil War sites like Pea Ridge, Arkansas? Families were not immune to the anxiety. Susie was worried about getting too far away from her ailing mom. I lucked out. They needed a cop at Yosemite and I got the gold-plated assignment. Cleve was also lucky and was off to Ohanapecosh Ranger Station at Mount Rainier National Park in Washington State.

Some were not as fortunate. Cliff Soubier went to Homestead National Monument near Omaha and wrote to us that he had to walk around in cow manure in the morning so he could be a part of the living history program. PJ Ryan, the drollest person I know, went to the South Entrance Station at Petrified Forest

National Park and told us it was the worst assignment for a bachelor in any national park. PJ converted his disgust with having to unload stolen petrified wood from a large percentage of the cars leaving the park into evenings writing and publishing *Thunderbear,* an alternative newsletter for park rangers.

I was very happy with my assignment. But I asked Wayne Cone, the center superintendent, why they hadn't sent me to the vacant position for a ranger at Kalapana on the coast of Hawai'i Volcanoes National Park. The station is about fifteen miles from my father's birthplace. He told me that it would cost the service a lot of money to ship my family over, and if I failed to make it through the one-year probation period they'd have to send us all back to San Jose at government expense. He also said that Yosemite was very interested in my California Peace Officer Certification. The fellow who got the Hawai'i assignment only lasted a short time. I have heard that his wife hated Hawai'i.

CHAPTER 4

Yosemite Christmas 1966

There may not be a more beautiful place to spend Christmas than Yosemite Valley. On Christmas Eve of 1966 we drove into the valley in the dark and were shown to a room in the Rangers' Club. It is a wonderful rustic old lodge that was built by Stephen Mather, the first director of the Park Service. Mather was a wealthy man who had made his fortune mining borax in Death Valley. He had the place built with his own money so rangers, who weren't paid much, had a place to stay. Rangers Tom Wylie and Don Utterback had been assigned to Yosemite from my ranger class as well. There was a fire going in the big stone fireplace and we made cocoa and gathered with the children around the fire feeling how lucky we were. In the morning we got up and walked out to see the wonderland we would be charged with caring for.

Often while we wait in dentists' and doctors' offices we see the familiar images of large-format prints made by Ansel Adams. Mr. Adams referred to the valley as "The Range of Light." The prints of Half Dome and Yosemite Falls are icons of American culture. They celebrate what is perhaps our peoples' greatest gift to themselves and their descendants: the national parks. Ansel Adams was able to use the values of black, white, and gray to tell the story of this magnificent glacier-carved valley, to fire our imaginations and make our hearts beat strong toward the protection and preservation of the landscape of America.

What we saw when we walked outside was the reality of all those Ansel Adams images we had been seeing for years. Ice had formed on the sides of Yosemite Falls during the night, and the ice broke off when warmed by the sun and it cascaded down, making sounds like big guns going off. It was a jaw dropper. You can come away from Yosemite Valley with a stiff neck from looking up at the wonders surrounding you.

We were assigned a house just outside the park boundary at El Portal. The NPS had developed a modern housing area complete with a grade school in an attempt to alleviate the crowded conditions in the valley. We moved in and I put on the flat hat and reported for duty.

Arch Rock — January 1967

I was assigned to run the entrance station at Arch Rock. This picturesque station sits right next to the cascades of the Merced River. In 1967 it was a four-hour drive from San Francisco and six hours from downtown Los Angeles, and on good-weather weekends as many as 10,000 people would come through the station on their way to make up part of the 30,000 to 40,000 people in Yosemite Valley. My seasonal rangers and I collected tens of thousands of one-dollar entrance fees and often worked our way through three lanes of cars entering the park with miles-long backups on the steep grade of Highway 140.

Today, when I go to parks on busy days and see many entrance stations abandoned and replaced by "iron ranger" slots to accept our money, I realize that one of the tenets of park management has changed. There is a lot of evidence that crime is lower in areas with staffed entrances. Ne'er-do-wells reckon that they will be observed during their escape and I believe it modifies their behavior. A visible ranger may not prevent all crime, but it makes people think twice.

The Arch Rock road was constructed during the time when most motor homes and recreational vehicles were seen on the pages of *Popular Mechanics* rather than on the narrow twisting pavement that came up from Mariposa. There is a short stone wall on the river side, and enormous granite stone blocks stick out over the road, causing worry in the minds of uninitiated drivers. Many straddle the center line on this picturesque drive and cause subsequent terror in the drivers coming the opposite direction. If you have ever seen the hilarious Lucille Ball and Desi Arnaz film *The Long Long Trailer*, you will know what the grades are like on Yosemite's roads.

Today's rangers drive purpose-made vehicles with sophisticated equipment and emergency components. In 1967 our only vehicle at Arch Rock was a 1964 Chevrolet half-ton pickup with a six-cylinder engine. On the dashboard some wag had put a plastic label that said, "Warning! If you go more than 45, remember this vehicle was furnished by low bid." There was a big rotating emergency light on the roof, and an old-fashioned mechanical siren under the hood. If you turned them both on at the same time, you couldn't go more than 45 anyway because of the voltage drop. On one occasion the cheap battery blew up from all the pressure. Nevertheless, this vehicle got us to burning cars, collisions, medical aid calls, and on more than one occasion carried arrestees to the "Old West" stone jail in Yosemite Valley.

Modern drivers don't know about vapor lock, the interruption of fuel in an internal combustion engine caused by bubbles in the fueling system due to heat. With a line of air-conditioned cars sitting on the steep entrance road on a hot day, the curse of vapor lock would come calling. The excess heat in the engine compartment would heat the fuel to a gaseous state before it got to the carburetor and starved the engine, causing it to die. Until it cooled back to a liquid, you couldn't restart the car. Meanwhile, the kids would be crying and a few impatient people back in the line would be blowing their horns. The seasonal college students who worked the station had a lot of experience with this. Some would grab an ice bag from the station fridge and go to the offending car, rub the ice bag on the fuel lines, and get the car started. One of the rangers even invented a device that you could clamp onto the carburetor stack and, using a hand pump, depressurize the system breaking the vapor lock.

On one hot day, an inbound car caught fire and an outbound motorist reported the fire to the service station in El Portal. They called me and I loaded the big fire extinguisher into the pickup, hit the siren and red lights and started down the hill. As I approached the car I saw two things: smoke pouring out from under the hood, and the driver and his family standing behind the vehicle waving frantically. It was at that moment I discovered that the brakes on the pickup were no better than the electrics. With my foot stamping on the brake pedal, I sailed past the whole shebang hearing the frazzled driver screaming, "Stop! Stop!" I yelled out the window, "I'll be right back!" Once I finally stopped, I backed up to the car and shot the fire extinguisher into the burning engine compartment.

The El Portal area had a fire truck that had been designed by committee. It was a heavy-duty pickup truck loaded with water and equipment that should have been on a two-ton chassis. The pump was mounted on the front of the bumper and was so heavy that the whole business handled cornering like a bear on roller skates. In the event of a fire we drove it well under the speed limit with siren blaring. As if this wasn't sufficient, someone ordered a foam educator like the ones used on airfields for extinguishing fuel fires. There was a petroleum "bulk plant" that held all the gasoline and diesel fuel for the gas stations in the park and we were told to go there in the event of a fire and shoot foam on it. Had that happened we would probably be blown across the valley. The foam was some kind of protein-based product and we practiced shooting it onto the hillside near our houses. During the following few days the place was visited frequently by cougars and coyotes that smelled something they liked in the foam.

Big-Time First Aid

I had learned about triage in my army training and later while working busy districts as a deputy sheriff. I had never had to deal with more than two injuries at a time, but I knew the concepts. The practice is something altogether different from the theory. On a busy day a car, straddling the center line above the Arch Rock Station, rammed into an upbound bus carrying a load of senior citizens. The bus broke through the stone wall and its right front wheel was hanging over the Merced River Gorge. I was the only one on duty at the time and called in on the radio for assistance as I got to the wreck. The driver got the front door opened and with my little first-aid kit, I jumped from a projecting rock onto the bus.

What I saw shocked me. There were many injured people. Without any restraints, elderly passengers, some with fragile bones, had been thrown around and there were broken bones and heavy bruising. Some people were on the floor. There was a lot of moaning and there were cries for help. I made my way down the aisle, checking for vital signs and traumatic shock first and then started working on the worst injuries. The driver got the back emergency door open, and by then, other help had arrived and we spent a couple of hours splinting broken bones, patching up small wounds, and evacuating ambulatory people and others on litters. Everyone on the bus survived, at least until they went home, but I learned a lot. Treating the elderly for traumatic shock is as important as taking care of non–life-threatening wounds. Telling people they have to wait is not much fun but it is necessary.

Some of the work was pretty grim, but there were those times when you could laugh. In winter we'd load sandbags in the pickup and it seemed as if we were constantly putting on and taking off tire chains. One night I was patrolling during a blizzard and came upon some tail lights cocked over at a weird angle. The car they belonged to had driven off the road and was high-centered on a rock. Only one side was in contact with the road and the other rear wheel was going around and around. I figured someone had suffered a heart attack or something so I flipped on the red lights, radioed in, and got out and ran up to the driver's door. Inside were two drunks and the one driving was looking out the nearly snow-covered windshield into a whiteout, thinking his car was still going somewhere. When I rapped on his window and he looked out and saw me, he nearly had a heart attack for real. He thought I was running alongside! He spent the rest of the night in the lockup. Drunk driving is not a laughing matter. But along with vigilance it does take a sense of humor to do law enforcement.

The Bravest Boy

He was a teenager, maybe fifteen at the time, and he had been afflicted with, I believe, polio. He was fitted with a big brace on one leg. The kid was smart, likable, and with a pronounced limp and an easy manner. His dad, Nick Arms, was on the staff of the park. I was working a night shift and was at home during a beautiful day when the phone rang and I was called to a rescue. The site was just a couple of hundred yards from my house and so I pulled on boots, grabbed a rope and first-aid kit, and ran down to the edge of the Merced River.

At El Portal, the Merced River rushes by with a full load of water coming down from the high country. It pours out of cascades and runs down through the park and miles below to a series of impoundments where it is stored and metered out for various uses. Formerly a stream with one of the southernmost runs of salmon and other anadromous fish, the river was so overcommitted there was no longer any water getting into the San Joaquin River and on to the ocean.

All of those beautiful waterfalls we marvel at were feeding the river on that day, and it was running high and cold. Out in the middle, in a swift current, clinging onto a flat five- or six-foot granite boulder, was the Arms boy hanging on in the fast current. On the rock in front of him was his five- or six-year-old brother. I scrambled down the twenty-foot embankment and uncoiled my rope.

Bob Dunnigan, the El Portal supervisory ranger, and Nick Arms, the boy's father, accompanied by a couple of other men, showed up with rescue gear. We rigged Nick up with a flotation jacket, strapped him into a harness, and put him into the river, upstream from the boulder. It took a while, but he was finally able to reach his boys, get them attached to his harness and pendulum through the current to the shore of the river. Nick was chilled but still functioning and carried his younger boy up the scramble route to the top. The older boy, however, was unable to stand. His skin had a blue look to it and he could not speak. We wrapped him in a blanket, strapped him onto my back, and I climbed up the embankment and got him to my house, where we could warm him.

After he could talk, he recounted their story. The two had been on the shore doing what boys do. I can't recall if they were fishing or just skipping rocks, but at one point the younger boy slipped and fell in. Without hesitation, his brother went in after him, got a grip on him, and was promptly washed out in the current, where he caught onto the boulder and yelled for help. Somehow he pushed his brother up onto the smooth boulder and hung on in the swift current until his father got to them.

After the boys were warmed up and examined by the doctor, I talked to the older boy and learned some lessons about bravery. Had he hesitated at all, his brother would have been washed away. The boy's metal brace on his leg must have weighted him down in the rushing water and, given the glacier and snowfield origins of the water, hypothermia could have caused him to lose his grip and his life. In my years as a ranger, I never encountered a braver person.

CHAPTER 5

The Valley—1967

The summer had begun and the crime rate in Yosemite Valley began its annual rise. It was, after all, the 1960s and someone had passed the word around the Haight-Ashbury that Yosemite was the place to be. Having done my rookie duty at Arch Rock, I was transferred to the Valley District. On Memorial Day we estimated that 37,000 people were cheek by jowl in the seven square miles of Yosemite Valley. Some of those park visitors were high on everything from cheap wine to LSD and so many joints were butted out in Stoneman Meadow (yes, that was the name) that the following spring I was told there was a minor crop of hemp to be harvested. I arrested drunk fraternity boys, who claimed, "Hey man, we're not 'heads,' we're 'juicers.' " I arrested drug sellers, drunk drivers, petty thieves, and assorted people for assault and battery. The superintendent sent Darryl Steele and me to San Francisco to meet with the staff of the Haight-Ashbury Free Clinic to get information on dealing with serious drug overdoses.

Since 1966 there have been homicides, armed robberies, and just about every kind of felony in this beautiful park. My account shouldn't scare anyone away. It's still a lot safer in Yosemite than where most of us live. It just seemed out of sync with the grandeur of the place. I had my first horseback patrol experiences during those chaotic days as well. When the valley was gridlocked with auto traffic, we could get to emergencies easier by wading the Merced River on horseback and riding cross-country to give help. Ranger Steele was our instructor; he had been a rider on the college rodeo circuit. The maximum the park was allowed to pay for a horse was $200, and we all believed the mounts were purchased from a breeder of cheap bucking rodeo horses.

My family and I now resided in a small house built by the US Army in the early days of the park. The downside was that park visitors would sometimes walk into your living room without invitation and say, "I just wanted to see how the rangers live." It was nothing to have people peer into the windows at any time the shades weren't pulled. The upside, however, was worth it. I could sit on the porch with Susie after work and enjoy a spectacular view of Yosemite Falls. The children attended school in the valley and their days off were filled with hiking and play in one of the best places possible.

Guns and Amphetamines Don't Mix

One evening, I was off duty splitting wood for our fireplace when a ranger car driven by a seasonal ranger pulled up and told me there was a report that someone had been shooting in the climbers' camp near Yosemite Falls. We did not carry weapons at the time. Some old revolvers were in a safe at the headquarters, but they weren't of much use. So off I went in jeans and a sweatshirt. When we arrived at the camp entrance, Ranger Tom Wylie and a seasonal ranger had blocked the entrance and were talking with three occupants of a car. I was told one man had chased the other two, firing a pistol at them. As carefully as I could, I sidled up to the open passenger window and heard the occupant say, "I'm gonna kill me a cop."

As he reached into the glove box, I reached in the open window, followed his hand into the box with my own and didn't find a gun. I yelled at the rangers to get the other two out on the ground, bent the arm of the fellow I had been grappling with out the window and opened the car door. Out came a six-foot-five man who was high on amphetamines and a lot of vodka. And he was fighting mad. As a young teen I had been taught judo by my uncle John but had not practiced for a few years. Somehow, the skills found their way back into me and I performed the best throw I had ever done, driving the fellow into the dirt and choking him into unconsciousness. With no handcuffs, I removed my belt and bound his wrists behind him.

While I was puffing out a gallon of adrenaline, a man stepped out of the darkness and said, "I'm a physician. Does he need any help?" By now the guy on the ground had regained consciousness, and I said, "No. But I sure as hell do." I had the rangers sit on the man on the ground while I searched the car. A .38 Special Colt revolver was under the seat the man had been sitting on. Fortunately, in his intoxicated state he had forgotten where he had put it. He had recently been released from prison and was on parole for bank robbery. He and his two friends were camping out and had gotten into an argument. He had chased them through the crowded camp, shooting wildly at them and, fortunately for them and the other campers, he was a lousy shot. In the morning US marshals came and hauled the sorry character back to prison.

The upshot of the event turned out to have significant fallout. I was called to testify before the federal grand jury in Fresno. They found it incredible that such goings-on took place in Yosemite. They were also skeptical about the common drug use in the park. In the 1960s it was everywhere. I was surprised at their incredulity.

In the same week my report showed up in the superintendent's office, another unexpected event took place. An abusive husband chased his wife through the maze of offices in the old headquarters building and ended up pushing her into the office of John Davis, the park superintendent, and beating the poor woman on the superintendent's desk. After pursuing rangers corralled the perpetrator, Mr. Davis, a calm and unruffled man in almost any circumstance, started making noise about the dreary state of law enforcement in the park.

The National Park Service was having growing pains. A patrol ranger at Point Reyes National Seashore had been murdered by a poacher while on night patrol by himself. "Should rangers be armed?" was the debate question going on from the director's office in Washington, DC, to the smallest park in the country. Someone in the Washington office sent two psychologists to interview me about the campground scuffle. One of their questions was framed like this: "Why would you need a pistol? You managed to subdue the person without one." I was flabbergasted. I told them that not one other patrol ranger had been a law enforcement officer for six years prior to becoming a ranger. None I knew of had judo training and hardly any had done personal combat with people bent on killing them. Most of the combat war veterans on the staff were supervisors and not out patrolling at night.

Slowly, change began to take place in the training and qualifications of park rangers. Sadly, the old pattern of rangers, the Swiss army knives of government, men and women who could give a sophisticated lecture on paleontology and an hour later rescue someone who had fallen while rock climbing, started to disappear. Today, you may be struck by the incongruity of rangers with full police gear. Some will be stationed in areas of high traffic and crime problems, while others, driving all-out four-wheel-drive police vehicles, may be found sitting alongside a remote road in an Alaskan park waiting for phantom speeders.

Having worked with small arms most of my career, I can't argue with arming rangers. My instincts tell me it was better in the old times, but we were just lucky. Firearms were not as common and were prohibited in the parks unless carried by law enforcement people, or sealed so they couldn't be used. Congress, in one of its less-enlightened moments, changed that law. Now, more loaded firearms are found in crowded campgrounds and tourist sites. Just a few years ago, Ranger Margaret Anderson was murdered at Mount Rainier National Park by a crazed gunman. The problem of guns in the hands of mentally disturbed people is greater than just a national parks issue. It will require some new thinking and some intestinal fortitude on the part of our legislators.

Adjusting to the Park Service

One day my children came home from the elementary school with information that didn't seem appropriate for a public school. Their teacher had lectured them about their behavior. He told them that they shouldn't dance because dancing was the initial move toward the sex act. My wife Susie paid a visit and the teacher was instructed that Sunday school couldn't be practiced between Monday and Friday in the public schools.

A similar event took place at another park I was assigned to. The children brought home "comic" books, supplied by their teacher, which portrayed the hell they were assigned to in the event they were not born again. For some reason the public schools near the parks seemed to draw from the wacky end of fundamentalist Christian teachers. I wanted my children to be able to read, write, balance their checkbooks, and think critically. I left their choice of what to believe about the spiritual world up to them.

In many ways the culture of the park staffs was similar to that of the military. One supervisor told me I needed to play bridge or I wouldn't get ahead in the Park Service. But that era was ending. Just as it was in the rest of the country, the Vietnam War was taking the children of the park employees and sending them home in boxes. It seemed there were no national parks that didn't experience funerals and memorial services or the endless waiting for those missing in action. The entire country was changing and park staffs were changing as well.

There were weddings and births in the parks and the people in the park communities were there when someone had trouble. The parks seemed like a social microcosm of small-town America. There was the good and there was the bad. On one occasion, an off-duty ranger had been sipping some whiskey during a pleasant afternoon when his pregnant wife began having contractions. The baby wasn't waiting the full nine months, and his father-to-be was in no shape to drive. So I was charged with driving the twisty road to the hospital for thirty minutes or so while hoping the little guy would wait just a little longer before making his debut. He did.

The big population of African-Americans, Hispanic-Americans, and most of the other hyphen Americans was pretty much absent from the park staffs. Most park people's knowledge of Hawai'ian culture was of Don Ho singing "Tiny Bubbles." Long overdue change was coming, if ever so slowly.

The Director Calls

I was the duty ranger on a busy summer Saturday when I got the call. "Hello," the caller said. "This is George Hartzog."

I couldn't believe it! It was the director of the Park Service himself, and he was calling on a Saturday! I said, "What can I do for you sir?"

"Let me speak to the superintendent," he said.

"He's off today, sir," I replied.

"Well, let me speak to the assistant superintendent," he said.

I gave the same answer as he went through the list of administration. It looked something like this:

Superintendent

    Assistant Superintendent

        Chief Ranger

            Assistant Chief Ranger

                District Ranger

                    Assistant District Ranger

                        Sub-District Ranger

"So who's in charge there today?" asked the top dog in the Park Service to the bottom dog.

"I am," I replied and we had a nice conversation on the telephone.

The call was noted in the log, and on Monday morning I was called in to explain to several people on the list what the director had said. "Sounded like a social call to me," I said. It hadn't been. The following week, a duty roster showed up and the brass who had been enjoying weekends off for some time were called to perform their duty on the days when most of the action took place. I never heard from other parks about the weekend duty rosters, but among the low-level rangers, the director, who was a distant figure to most of us, went way up in our estimation.

Campers

One evening, I was driving a patrol vehicle, accompanied by one of the experts on Yosemite's famous tree crew. These Native American men were specialists at diagnosing and removing trees that threatened concentrations of park visitors. Trees with internal rot would fall on cabins and campgrounds in the parks and sometimes injure or even kill people. These experts were sent everywhere in the west when they were needed and I never saw a more capable bunch. They could lay a big tree down between two obstacles or buildings without any problem at all.

As we drove by one of the campgrounds, we observed an enormous campfire surrounded by a dozen or so senior citizens in folding chairs. The flames nearly touched the remaining lower limbs on a tree. Campers were prohibited from cutting limbs or using downed branches for their campfires, but they did anyway. My companion observed, "White man fire." It was actually the first time I had heard the term. He explained, "You could shoot a cannon through here fifteen feet above the ground and never touch a limb." To procure branches and twigs to burn, people would stand on top of vehicles to cut the limbs. We walked into the campground and had the campers moderate the blaze down to just a big fire instead of a dangerous conflagration. When we drove away, the tree guy said, "Indians would never build a fire that big. It's too much work for just cooking, and your enemies could see it for fifty miles."

The camping I had been doing all my life had been relatively minimal as far as equipment went. Things were transitioning to today's camping, which seems to be split between folks with enormous recreational vehicles complete with generators and all the comforts of home, and the antithesis: minimalist campers using very expensive and sophisticated backpacking and camping gear. But in the late 1960s we were seeing more and larger trailers and truck-mounted campers, and I discovered an interesting thing. People drove into the campgrounds and set up their stuff. At that point I would expect them to take a stroll into an open spot and have a look at the magnificent scenery they had spent a day in traffic for. But no—after setting up they walked around the campground comparing what they had with everyone else's stuff. And then came discussions over cups of coffee about the latest equipment or what someone else had adapted so his rig worked better.

It wasn't just the RV people. The rock-climbing folks in the climbers' camp were examining pitons, carabiners, and the newest high-tech climbing ropes while they passed around jugs of cheap wine. I discovered what I called "camper tribes." The Airstream trailer bunch would gather in one place, and backpackers in another. Sometimes the gatherings were highly organized. I've seen nearly an entire campground in a park filled with unusual compact trailers called Casitas. The license plates would be from everywhere in the US and Canada. Trailer owners had planned this gathering so they could be with their tribe.

Another kind of tribe showed up in the mid-1960s. On January 14, 1967, tens of thousands of young people attended the first "Be In" at Golden Gate Park in San Francisco. Owsley Stanley supplied thousands of participants with LSD, and they heard from Timothy Leary who advised them to "Tune in, turn on, and drop out." After the performances by rock bands the Grateful Dead, Big Brother and the Holding Company, and Jefferson Airplane, someone must have suggested that they drop out in Yosemite Valley, because the invasion began just three weeks after I showed up for my first assignment.

Some hitchhiked in, carrying only a blanket and prepared to live off the land. Some ended up living off other campers, and food thefts were common. Others came in every kind of conveyance. One group had turned a Volkswagen bus into a huge fiberglass bathtub. It was a legal conveyance with all the required lights and mirrors and a rudimentary windshield. With the exception of the driver who had a bucket seat, the campers all sat facing one another around the "fur-lined" bathtub. How I wish I had taken a photograph! One guy in a VW Bug had a huge St. Bernard and told me he didn't need a sleeping bag; the dog kept him warm. The band Three Dog Night was popular during those years, and we heard their music a lot.

Rangers could never guess what was going to show up next. There were territorial disputes over who was entitled to the seven square feet between that stump and someone's tent. Arguments over noise were pretty common. Children were lost and found. There was food left on tables just waiting for a bear to have lunch. Cars needed jump starts. And exhibitionists having nighttime sex had to be asked to turn off the lantern inside their tent so the teenagers gathered together for X-rated shadow entertainment could be sent back to their campsites. I may have had lots of issues with these visitors, but I must admit that it was entertaining,

I was walking through a campground early one morning when a big pickup camper blew up. The top of the aluminum structure peeled open like a sardine can and a man in a bathrobe flew out the back, not fifty feet in front of me. He was holding onto a match that had ignited the thing. Inside the now-open camper was a woman who had flash burns on her body, along with melted nylon from her sleep garment. Other than burns, the flying man had landed uninjured. The hospital was only a few hundred yards away, and I got them transported quickly for burn treatments. When I interviewed the man, I discovered that it was the second day of his retirement and he had picked up the brand-new camper in the Bay Area the day before and had not lit the stove until just before the explosion occurred.

The camper itself was towed to an area near the firehouse and I worked it over to find what had caused the explosion. The man had been burned only on his bare legs and the woman, who had been lying on her side in a low bed, had burns only on the uncovered side. Propane gas is heavier than air and when it leaks, it gathers from the floor upward. The camper door had a window slightly opened for ventilation and the propane had leaked out the opening after it pooled up about two feet deep. When the man lit his match, the camper top blew open, but the burns were confined to the lower area. I pressurized the system with air and brushed thick soapy water on the junctions and found a leaking connection that had been cross threaded.

My report prompted a lawsuit and later that year I received a Christmas card from the couple with a $50 check enclosed. I showed it to the chief ranger and posted it back to the couple with a nice note and an explanation that we couldn't take gratuities. A week later, a huge box of See's chocolates showed up in the ranger office mail with no return address. I could tell by the postmark where it had come from, but we all ate the chocolates anyway.

Dangling from Granite Walls

No one ever said it, but terror has to be kept under control if you are the person others are depending on to get them off the ridiculously difficult places they have gotten to on Yosemite's sheer granite walls. The valley was known as the university for rock climbers. Yvon Chounard, the founder of Patagonia Clothing and the designer of some of the first truly engineered climbing hardware, was climbing at Yosemite in those days, as was Royal Robbins, who also founded a successful outdoor clothing company.

Young people from all over came to try their skills on everything from twenty-foot high boulders to big walls. Really big walls. I had heard that Supervisory Ranger Rick Anderson had been part of the group that had first conquered the previously unclimbable Nose Route on El Capitan in the 1950s. Rick was now the lead on the rock rescue team. His feet had been frostbitten when he had served in the Korean War and that made it difficult for his toes to feel the rocks when climbing. But he was tough. When he asked me to take rock-climbing training and join the rescue group, I was astounded. Who would want to be roped up to a 215-pound Hawai'ian while climbing one of these walls?

It turned out they needed ballast and strength. I was the guy who belayed everyone else from the base of the climb and then was the last one up and belayed some more up the next pitch and so forth. You tie me to a tree or stable rock, and I pay out rope as you climb and if you fall, you go past the last anchor you have installed on your way up, and I run the rope around my rear end and put the brakes on so you go no further. For some reason I also had an ability to calm those people we rescued. Most were just inexperienced guys who free climbed up this rock and along that ledge and then discovered that going down the route they had ascended, without a rappel rope, was a whole lot harder than coming up.

Some of the seasonal rangers were good climbers and they took me on some difficult climbs. I managed to do them, but can't say I was ever enamored of the sport. I participated in many rescues and searches, including evacuations of bodies of people who had taken the big plunge. There was no toxicological evidence, but statements by onlookers led us to believe that some of the deaths were caused by drug use distorting the judgment of the victims. The park's expert climbers did the serious technical rescues of climbers injured or stuck on the big walls, but there were many more inexperienced climbers who got in trouble in the lower reaches, and those were the rescues I participated in.

On one lovely summer afternoon, the Fresno Symphony Orchestra came to Yosemite Valley to give a concert in the meadow just outside the Ahwahnee Hotel. I was on nights, so we farmed out the children and Susie packed a picnic lunch and a bottle of wine and off we went to hear Respighi's *Pines of Rome* performed under the pines of Yosemite. Just as the music started and the cork was pulled, however, a seasonal ranger hurried across the meadow and reported a climber stuck on a ledge above the Nevada Falls Trail.

Leaving the lovely music and the lovely wife, I was dropped off at the rescue cache where seasonal ranger-climbers awaited. After a quick change and swapping loafers for a pair of climbing boots, we drove to the trail head and hurried up the trail toting a Stokes litter and all the ropes and hardware we thought we might need. Curious crowds are usually present at these events and can sometimes be a problem. This crowd, however, was quietly watching a ledge a couple of hundred feet up above. We could hear the fellow calling but couldn't see him. So we roped up and made the ascent in three or four pitches until we got to the ledge everyone had been pointing at.

The ledge turned out to be big enough for fifty people to have a picnic on, but the traumatized climber was all the way at the back of the ledge and the reason we had not been able to see him from below became obvious. The intrepid novice climber was prone with his arm jammed down in a crack. "Are you stuck?" I asked.

"No!" he shouted. "I'm not taking my arm out until you guys rope me up." We tried to get a rescue harness on the terrified guy, but it wasn't working.

"Pull your arm out!" I called out.

Again he refused, saying, "Not until you rope me up."

Exasperated, and uptight for having to give up a romantic afternoon to deal with this guy, I said, "That's not the point. The cracks in the back of these ledges are where the rattlesnakes hang out during the heat of the day."

The prospect of unseen rattlesnakes outdid his other worries and he hurriedly yanked his arm out. We got him roped up and rappelled down the cliff with him. As we hiked down the trail we heard the last strains of the orchestra's final selection drifting through the trees.

Biker Invasion

An Oakland Police Department intelligence officer called us in early July and told us that a "rumble" was coming our way from the San Francisco Bay Area. The Hell's Angels were due at the Forest Service campground at Bass Lake outside Yosemite's south boundary. The East Bay Dragons from Oakland were supposed to be coming up for a battle on the Fourth of July, but nobody knew where it was to take place. But sure enough, the Dragons came rumbling into our Wawona campground and took over a substantial part of it. We were all issued hard hats and riot batons and put on standby in case the war started in the park.

Tom Hartman, who was the district ranger at the south entrance, had a better idea. Tom hooked the big bear-trap trailer onto his pickup and drove into the campground. The trap was a heavy length of steel culvert pipe with a big iron door that cranked up on tracks and was set with a trigger inside. The bear would climb in to get the food tied to the trigger and the door would come down with a huge bang. Then the ranger would drive the trailer somewhere remote and release the bear. Tom parked the trap near the Dragons' camp and climbed up in the truck bed. He cranked open the heavy iron trap door and then let it fly. It made a loud clanging noise when it shut and he drew an audience.

"What's this?" asked one of the bikers.

"Rogue bear," Tom said. The bikers, who spent their nights in the open, promptly kickstarted their choppers and hit the road out of the park. They were willing to get into it with the Hell's Angels, but not Tom's phantom rogue bear.

Later that summer, a group of outlaw bikers rumbled into Yosemite Valley and blocked one of the old stone bridges. Traffic backed up for a mile or so while they had a smoke. Five or six rangers ordered them to get moving and the group, which numbered twenty or so, just laughed.

It was a standoff until we looked down the empty outgoing lane and spotted the district ranger driving a big truck with a huge steel screw-type snow blower on the front. During the previous winter, I had seen that machine eat the first eighteen inches of a Ford Falcon that had slid into it during a whiteout. The ranger had a demented look on his face and as he approached, he turned on the device and the big parallel screws, designed to chew up ice and snow, started their noisy turning. The smiles on the bikers' faces vanished when they realized that he didn't intend to stop and meant to chew up some Harleys. They tossed their cigarettes and ran for the bikes. Those who couldn't get them started on the first kick were last seen pushing their bikes at a fast run and we never saw them again.

CHAPTER 6

Bears

For many years, an area near Camp Curry was used as a dump. Later, responding to the growth in trash, the dump was closed and the garbage was hauled out of the park. A transfer station had replaced the old dump, but generations of black bears had been using the dump for a long time and they had taught their offspring to visit it. So when the bears came sniffing around the dumpsters at night, there would be dozens of flashes going off from cameras of visitors looking for wildlife shots to take home. I have no idea how many people watched slide shows that included pictures of these black bears trying to get into secured dumpsters. Rangers had to referee the nightly dumpster jamboree to keep the players apart. The bears became more adept at getting food every year and raided campsites and cars on a regular basis. The issue was exacerbated by fools who fed the bears in order to get a photo.

At that time, the bear population of Yosemite Valley was estimated at just under forty. Interactions with visitors became a serious problem and severe claw wounds were not uncommon. We were required to kill the bears that attacked and injured visitors. We knew some of the bears on a personal-name basis; they had been named by seasonal employees. I was tasked with euthanizing the bear known as "El Cid." He had clawed a pair of teenagers who had waded to a wooded island to get some privacy, and as a result, the pair were suffering from a bad case of *Ursus Interruptus*.

Two seasonal rangers and I began to follow the big male bear through the campgrounds. I carried a .375 caliber Weatherby magnum rifle designed for killing large animals. Killing a bear with a big gun without endangering someone in our filled-up campgrounds and lodges was not an easy task. All afternoon and evening we followed the big bear until about ten at night, when we finally found a place to take the shot. The bear had decided to wade across the Merced River downstream from Stoneman Bridge. We had followed him through Camp Seven, and from up on the bank I could shoot at a downward angle with the opposite bank as an effective backstop.

My father had taught me to shoot when I was a young teen. I was an expert marksman. But this was a difficult shot. The bear was in the water moving away and the rangers' flashlights were wavering as the two seasonal rangers were breathing hard. I was also puffing a little from the jogging pursuit and needed a brace-rest to get the shot. The closest rest was the side of a small Airstream trailer in a campsite right above the river. I braced against the trailer, calmed my breathing, and found the bear in the telescopic sight.

The Weatherby has a big cartridge and it makes a hellacious loud noise when you fire it. When the rifle went off, the poor fellow asleep inside the aluminum and wood trailer had a terrible awakening. *Boom!* went the rifle. I cranked another round in as the bear rose up and spun around twice and then dropped into the shallows. The first shot had been true. The awakened camper popped his head out the door to see what was going on, and here was a ranger cloaked in gun smoke with a rifle yelling, "Get back inside!" He did.

I waded out with the rifle ready, but the shot had been placed correctly and the big bear was dead. We rousted several seasonal rangers out of their tent cabins and dragged the bear out of the river, up the bank, and into the pickup. I weighed the truck, drove the bear to the site we used to dispose of the carcasses, and went back and weighed the truck again. It's a rough estimate, but the bear weighed about 600 pounds and was the biggest Yosemite black bear I ever saw. And I hated having to kill him. In the morning I went back to apologize to the camper. He was okay with the whole deal, and before too long his hearing was back to normal and he was telling the story to all the other campers.

Not too long after that, a yearling bear clawed a visitor in another campground. Often a young bear will "tree" if pursued. This one did so. In order to avoid shooting a firearm upward in the crowded valley, we would use a tranquilizer dart loaded with Sucostrin. The metal syringe cylinder is shaped like a short cigar and is delivered either with an air rifle or a bow and arrow.

The thick-bore needle on the device injects the chemical on impact and will tranquilize the bear. This bear had sent a woman to the hospital for cleaning and stitching so, unfortunately, it had earned the death penalty. We loaded the cylinder with a lethal dose, and I used the bow and arrow device and shot the dart into the bear's buttocks.

As the poor beast crashed down through the tree branches, a troop of Girl Scouts came out of the bushes behind us. Their leader was lecturing them, "The bear's not dead." She said, "He's just asleep. They're going to take him to some remote place and drop him off in the wild." The seasonal rangers looked at me for guidance. "Get the bear in the truck," I said. They did so and the children gathered around as I started for the cab and a quick getaway. It was not to be.

"Look!" one of the more observant girls said. "He's not breathing." The bear was dead but quivering from the effects of the drug on his nervous system. I ordered one of the rangers into the truck bed and said, "Pump on his chest." As I drove away I saw in my side-view mirror the skeptical look on the Scout leader's face. She knew the bear was dead—though why she would attempt to say otherwise in the first place I had no clue. Around a couple of corners I stopped to let the ranger back in the truck cab. "That was quick thinking," he said. "If it had lasted any longer you'd have been giving the bear mouth-to-mouth resuscitation," I replied.

Some of the seasonal rangers were smarter than others. These were mostly college students working as rangers during their summer breaks. All were intelligent but some had very little common sense. One fellow was asked to take a bear trap out to a problem location and set it away from the camping area. He said he knew how to work the thing, so off he went with the pickup and trailer. After a couple of hours of not hearing from him, I sent another guy to find out if he was having problems. He found the first ranger trapped inside the bear trap, and he was broiling in the summer heat. He didn't know what the little hatch in the front of the trap was for! Instead of baiting the trap through the little hatch and then cranking the winch that raised the big door up before returning to the hatch to set the trigger, he had entered the trap, hung the rotting bait on the hook and triggered the trap door shut on himself. We nearly had ourselves a baked ranger.

One quiet winter morning at three a.m. or so I got a call from the desk at the Ahwahnee Hotel. The excited night man was hollering into the phone that a bear had gotten into the hotel and was running around frantically trying to get out. The Ahwahnee is the "high end" of the Yosemite hotels. I rolled in and grabbed a shovel out of the back of the patrol wagon and went in the front door.

It turned out that the night shift baker had propped the kitchen door open so he could empty several containers of garbage without having to open the door each time. On one trip to the "bear-proof" dumpster, a medium-sized black bear had made its way into the kitchen.

When the baker went in for another load, the bear panicked and started to run around the kitchen, bellowing at the top of its lungs. The baker jumped up on the big grill and yelled for help. Hearing the commotion, the night man opened the door to the kitchen and was nearly bowled over by the bear as it barreled into the main lobby area.

By the time I showed up, the bear was in a large sun room, jumping onto the expensive furniture trying to find a way out. He had already pooped on the Navaho rugs and was in total bear-panic. I banged the shovel on the floor and advanced on the bear. It ran around the big fireplace and into the lobby, so I opened all the doors in the sun room and went after the bear. Soon the bear was after me and I backed around near one of the doors, and when the bear advanced with his hackles raised, I banged the shovel on the stones at the fireplace and he darted out one of the open doors.

I had to kill three bears during my tenure as a national park ranger and I hated every one of the experiences. It is one thing to hunt and kill an animal for food. It's quite another to have to take its life because people have gotten it used to handouts. Most of the bears had been fed either intentionally or through carelessness by ignorant park visitors. Feeding a bear is like being on a homicide jury and voting for the death penalty for the bear. A black bear is a creature of habit. Once the bear learns to get food it will return over and over to repeat the experience. Many of the bear incidents including some fatal attacks in other parks have been caused by bears that have gotten accustomed to garbage or camper food. To save these magnificent creatures and to save the rangers from the terrible duty required of them, the animals should be left alone and campers should use secure storage for their groceries.

CHAPTER 7

Yosemite's Hospital

Yosemite's Lewis Memorial Hospital was founded by the US Army in 1913. It was turned over to the Interior Department in 1915 and has been running full throttle ever since. With the exception of his service during World War II, Dr. Avery Sturm had run the hospital from 1935 until I met him in 1967. Dr. Sturm set more broken legs and stitched up more ski cuts than anyone I have heard of. His staff of doctors and nurses in the little six-room hospital treated bear clawings, traffic accident victims, and skiing injuries. I believe he could have set broken legs blindfolded. Park employees and their families depended on the staff for regular medical care. Some park families and visitors bore their children under his care and that of his medical staff and an excellent corps of nurses.

Other Duties as Assigned

I had been tagged as the park's police ranger and I was glad to be of service. But other adventures were waiting. I wanted to learn the ropes about being a complete ranger any way I could. Although I didn't mind the duty, being the designated police guy was not what I wanted to do forever. I took an interest in learning how to control minor wildfires, so I began hanging out at the fire cache, where crews were dispatched, on my days off and working as a crew member. I worked my way up to fire boss on a few fires. I ended up leading crews of ten or fifteen firefighters to some remote lightning-caused fires. The work was strenuous and it could be dangerous but ultimately it was very rewarding. The fire boss has to suppress the fire and bring his or her crew out alive and uninjured. It's a hell of a responsibility.

In the winter I was assigned weekends at Badger Pass, the park's ski area. My only experience in skiing was at a little area in Clare, Michigan, in the 1950s. Back then, traveling with a carload of Michigan State University students and a supply of cheap wine, I got on some ill-fitting rental boots and skis and rope-towed up a couple of pitches to the top of the mountain. My common sense told me it was a bad idea, but the wine spoke in a louder voice and I jumped off into something called "the nose dive."

It was aptly named. I fell at least five times before I got to the bottom and found some more gentle hills to slide down. Then I hid in the heated lodge for the remainder of the day to keep from killing myself.

At Yosemite, novice rangers got free ski lessons and discounted skis. I acquired a pair of laminated wood downhill racing skis that were stiff enough to handle my weight and I took lessons on my days off. Soon, I was jumping moguls and having a great time.

The duty days were different. We had to pass a test before we were allowed to be on duty on the slopes. We were required to climb from the bottom to the top of the ski area on our skis. We used sealskin strips strapped to our skis to get traction, and it took more than an hour of huffing and puffing to climb the hill. All of this was done in case the lifts broke down and we had to go up after injured skiers. When the ski patrol had too many injuries to deal with, rangers would pick up injured skiers and ski them down to the first-aid station on the Austrian Akja rescue sled.

Our other duties were to ski down under the chairlift and inspect it every morning, and to be the last skiers at the end of the day on every slope so no injured were left out there. But our most important duty was not on the slopes. We ran the first-aid station. On any busy weekend the ski patrol would bring us, on average, fourteen major injuries: blown-out knees, fractures, dislocations, major trauma from collisions, and cuts requiring more than six stitches. Some of the breaks were compound in nature, with bone fragments sticking through the skin. Occasionally, we'd get a rotated fracture where the ski boot was pointed backward.

Each day, before the injury parade started, the rangers would peel off a sheet of cardboard from our supply and use a carton cutter to form several sizes of folded leg splints someone had designed. They were like origami, but on a large scale. When skiers with simple fractures or damaged knees or ankles showed up, we'd leave their ski boots laced up, slide the cardboard under the leg, fold the thing up like a big cardboard boot and tape it onto the person's injured leg. The big metal Thomas traction splint, with all the adjustments and suspensions, was used for really serious leg fractures. One day, someone who had evidently flunked high school science, but wanting to introduce something he thought would be more efficient, brought in a new inflatable leg splint and put it on a broken leg. On the way down to Yosemite Valley in the ranger wagon, the victim started yelling. The elevation drop had caused the thing to deflate, causing extreme pain when the wagon would jostle, and the transporting ranger had to stop twice to blow the darned thing up.

I can't imagine a better place to learn to deal with serious injury. Dr. Sturm, down in Yosemite Valley, would get the patients out of the ambulance and set the bones or brace up the knee or stitch up the many edge cuts, caused by sharpened steel edges on skis. We learned how to talk to badly injured people. We never said things like, "You're going to be just fine," and we didn't give looks that said "Holy crap!" when we unpacked the temporary splints and worked on immobilizing the breaks. We learned that if you could just be calm, look the injured in the eye, and act like you knew what you were doing, there wasn't much chance that the injured would go into traumatic shock.

There were times when the injured person seemed relieved to get off the slopes. Perhaps they were only out there skiing because of peer pressure. Sometimes they might show up with the gang the following weekend and sit in the lodge with mulled wine while people wrote clever things on their leg casts.

Dr. Sturm taught us to shave around cuts and use butterfly closures to hold together the edge cuts. A fallen skier was sometimes skied over by the person trailing them. We'd bring them in, clean the wound with a green soap solution, shave and close it, and ship them down to Dr. Sturm. If we did it right, he'd stitch as he pulled off the temporary closures.

One day I was putting an elaborate device called an airplane splint on a woman who had dislocated her shoulder. She was in great pain. We couldn't reduce the separated joint, so we had to send her to the hospital and have the dislocation corrected, putting the bone end back in its socket. As we were dealing with this, a fellow walked in holding a towel to his face and said, "I got cut." I waved him over to a chair and told him to relax and I'd be with him after we got the woman strapped up to the splint. He did as I told him, and waited patiently.

Fifteen minutes later, we gingerly placed her in a ranger car. With that, I went back in and pulled the towel off the skier's face—and found out that someone had skied across his face. The cut went across his forehead, one eyebrow, had narrowly missed his eye and continued down his cheek. It looked awful, but he didn't complain. We got him on the treatment table and I cleaned the wound and shaved it. We must have used sixteen butterfly closures to get the edges together and then wrapped his head in a bandage that wouldn't stick to the whole shebang, and sent him on his way to the hospital.

Later, the telephone rang. It was Dr. Sturm, who started off the conversation with "Who's the moron who shaved off that guy's eyebrow?"

"You're speaking to him," I replied.

"How the hell was I supposed to line up his eyebrow? He's going to go through life with a lightning-streak eyebrow on one side unless I was really lucky."

I replied, "You told us to shave off the hair."

"Okay, put out a new order," Dr. Sturm said. "*Don't* shave off eyebrows. And watch out later in the season. If it comes out crooked and he's angry, I'm sending him to you."

Ski season was a busy time, but there was a fun event that we all looked forward to. Before the spring melt, rangers would ski into the back country and check snow depths. Reports from a series of regular geographic data points were transmitted to the State of California water management people who made plans for water releases designed to avoid flooding and to provide agricultural and municipal water supplies. Those were the ostensible reasons for the ski tours. The real reason was that we enjoyed a whiskey-fueled back-country tour where we could tell lies, bark at the moon, build igloos, sleep in snow caves, and just have one hell of a good time.

One snow survey involved being towed on skis all the way up to Tuolumne Meadows behind a Weasel snow tractor. Our job was to measure depths so the park management could plan for plowing to open the road across the 10,000-foot Tioga Pass. Snow drifts frequently exceeded ten feet. All of these winter trips were skied on surplus wooden US Army skis with old-fashioned bear-trap bindings. Today's rangers have much better equipment, but I'm willing to wager that they continue to take whiskey along on that trip.

Danger in the Parks

There is a human tendency to magnify bad news and to believe it only happens somewhere other than where we choose to live and recreate. Every tragic shooting is followed by newscasts in which the person interviewed says, "I just can't believe this has happened here. This kind of thing happens in Los Angeles or Detroit, not here!" The same is true about national parks. People do not want to believe in the inherent danger that is in the parks. During my service at Yosemite, there were twenty fatalities among the four million–plus visitors to the park. Of the twenty, three drowned, three died in motor vehicle crashes, one from a drug overdose, six from heart attacks, one from a pulmonary edema, one from an industrial accident, one from diving into shallow water, and six from falls. With the exception of the falls and the edema death, these statistics, while tragic, are not at all unusual for a moving population such as we see in the national parks. Each death was a tragedy and we would work hard to see what could be done to prevent accidents and deaths, but the numbers are probably lower than the death rate in a two-year period in the place you live. Only three of the deaths from falls were by people taking part in classic mountaineering.

On March 30, 1967, Larry Greene and Edwin Hermans, members of the Stanford Alpine Club, failed to return from a climb in the vicinity of Half Dome. It wasn't until June 18 that their bodies were found near Awiyah Point. One of the young men was found in the "self-arrest" position with his ice axe dug into the slope, while the other showed signs of rope burns, and the speculation was that they were caught in an avalanche. These climbers were well prepared and experienced, and were probably just unlucky. The tragedy came home to me when I discovered that the man weeping as we brought the body bag down to the valley was the father of one of the victims, Ernest Greene, my physics professor from San Jose State. The vision of that grieving parent stays with me to this day.

Another experienced climber fell into a notch near the base of the Lost Arrow, a spectacular pinnacle of granite that spikes upward next to Yosemite Falls. We were unable to recover his body without serious risk to the climbing team and we had to refuse the pleas of his parents to bring his remains down. A climbing priest rappelled down and blessed the body, but that was the best we could do. Other falls were from less-experienced people. One was evidently swimming in the pool above Yosemite Falls and was swept over the falls.

There is a part of each national park that calls out challenges. It says to leave the comfort of your home and trek into the wilderness carrying a backpack. It calls people to scale the granite walls, to shoot the rapids in a kayak or raft, to climb the tallest mountain in North America and all the lesser ones as well. "Test yourself against me," it cries. And thousands do. Many are prepared and take the challenge. Others are not and are largely lucky enough to get off with major frights and minor injuries. But there will always be a few who fail and pay the price. The National Park Service spends a lot of time training its employees and designing its facilities to keep visitors safe. Park rangers do their best to warn people, teach them skills, and when necessary save them from their mistakes, but nature always has a few surprises and once in a while they are fatal.

CHAPTER 8

Visitors

"Before many years, if proper facilities are offered, these hundreds will become thousands and in a century the whole number of visitors will be counted by millions. An injury to the scenery so slight that it may be unheeded by any visitor now, will be one of deplorable magnitude when its effect upon each visitor's enjoyment is multiplied by these millions. But again, the slight harm which the few hundred visitors of this year might do, if no care were taken to prevent it, would not be slight, if it should be repeated by millions. At some time, therefore, laws to prevent an unjust use by individuals of that which is not individual but public property, must be made and rigidly enforced." — Frederick Law Olmstead in a report to the California Legislature on the findings of the Yosemite Commission 1865

In 1864 President Lincoln, in an act that would portend the extensive system of state and national parks, granted Yosemite Valley and the Mariposa Grove of Giant Sequoias to the young State of California. African-American soldiers from the Ninth Cavalry of Buffalo Soldiers were the first to patrol Yosemite. In 1914 the park was taken back by the federal government and in 1916 was included in the new National Park System.

The earliest visitor statistics tell us that 369 visitors came to Yosemite on horseback or in horse-drawn conveyances in 1865. One hundred years later there were 1,635,380 and in 1967 the number had grown to 2,238,300. They came in buses, in cars, psychedelic painted VW vans, and towing every kind of vacation trailer. Many hitchhiked in and camped. In 2014, there were 4,029,416 visitors. Olmstead's prediction had come true.

A President Visits

Many Presidents of the United States and visiting dignitaries have visited Yosemite. I was assigned to a task force to protect President Cevdet Sunay of Turkey during his visit to the park. His motorcade had been threatened by Greek Cypriot demonstrators in New York and there had been bomb threats. We were told that President Sunay had come to the US for several diplomatic reasons. One was to fly to Independence, Missouri, to thank retired President Harry S Truman for his help in keeping the Soviet Union at bay. Another reason was more obscure. We were told that as a student, Cevdet Sunay had studied forestry. His lifelong desire had been to see, in person, a giant sequoia tree.

President Sunay was a gruff-looking man, barrel chested, and he was abrupt in his manner. He was taken to his suite at the Ahwahnee Hotel and a ranger was assigned to baby sit his limousine in a locked garage to avoid any potential bomb placement. As soon as he got to his room, he pushed the courtesy cart loaded with alcoholic beverages out into the hall and ordered the manager to bring him some fruit. He was a practicing Muslim. I spent the night seated on a stool in the wooded area outside the window of his room at the hotel with a shotgun across my lap and a security guard for company.

Bright and early the next morning, we were on our way in a caravan of cars out to the Mariposa Grove. The snow had been plowed, and park employees had shoveled a five- or six-foot deep path to and around the "Grizzly Giant," one of the park's more spectacular trees. The tree soars 210-feet high and its heavily buttressed trunk is thirty feet in diameter at its widest measurement.

I was stationed with other rangers keeping an eye out for trouble when the limousine pulled up. President Sunay stepped out of the car, fully dressed in a black morning coat complete with tails and a top hat. He took one look at the tree, shucked the morning coat and top hat, and wearing a dickey and T-shirt with dress shoes, he jogged to the tree and tried to hug it. He laughed his way all around the big tree, exclaiming something like *Ay ya yai!* over and over. Then he motioned us over, borrowed Ranger Norm Messinger's flat hat, placed it on his own head and posed for a picture with all of the rangers present. The serious-looking, gruff man had the biggest grin I had seen in a long time and he thanked each of us with a handshake before he climbed back in the car.

The July Fourth Riot

The summer after I left for my next assignment, the tension between park rangers and young people heated up. More people, fresh from reading Jack Kerouac's books *On the Road* and *The Dharma Bums*, armed with various chemical mood enhancers, sought the peace and spiritual refreshment offered in the national parks. Yosemite had the reputation of the place to go for such activity and it was in close proximity to the San Francisco Bay Area. The mixture of young alcohol-stupefied kids, motorcycle gangs, disapproving seniors, and families from Middle America mixed into the cauldron with the refugees from the Haight-Ashbury boiled over on July 4, 1970.

There are a few theories about why the whole thing started, but what transpired changed the Park Service. A collection of young people was hanging about in Stoneman Meadow. After a dustup during a Memorial Day weekend, rangers tightened the enforcement of camping rules and displaced many young people. They gathered in the meadow and defied the rangers who were sent to disperse the crowd. Park rangers, aided by deputized wranglers on horseback, arrived and tried to move the crowd. Things got out of hand and some of the mounted riders swung night sticks and knotted ropes to subdue the crowd. Angry young people responded with rocks and bottles and drove the makeshift Mounties from the meadow.

Reinforcements from area sheriffs' departments and other police were called in and the situation was brought under control. Someone filmed the whole thing and it became a counterculture cause, with criticism and support flying back and forth in the press and through letters to the Park Service. Many observers considered it a police riot.

Two things resulted. Park management started taking the law enforcement responsibility more seriously. Rangers and their horses received training on their use in patrol and crowd control. The Park Service even started a Morgan Horse farm at Point Reyes National Seashore in order to provide more appropriate mounts for the rangers and park police. Rangers were moved away from their generalist profile, and many became fully trained federal law enforcement officers.

The second thing that happened concurrently was what some considered major harassment of counterculture people. According to the July 25, 1971, edition of *The New York Times*, "National Parks: A report on the range war at generation gap," rangers were using profiling techniques to deny people entrance to Yosemite. An article by Jack Hope in the May 1971 edition of *Natural History* magazine laid out much the same argument, but the culture war extended far and wide in the parks, and only the passage of time and the maturing of people on both sides of the disputes seem to have healed many of the wounds.

The End of the Firefall

Every evening during the visitor season, the park concessioner held an event that was a part of the history of the park. Hundreds of people walked and drove to Camp Curry to witness a spectacular happening. Far above, on a ledge below Glacier Point, employees started a fire using red fir bark. An evening program, held in the amphitheater at Curry Village, would come to an end after entertainment and a ranger talk. (A friend told me his toughest gig was to give a glacier talk in between the belly dancer and the Firefall.)

As darkness fell, a man with a megaphone would come before the hushed crowd and shout, "The Stentor calls; hello, Glacier Point." A voice from the rim of the valley would call back, "Hello, Camp Curry." The megaphone person then would shout the command everyone was waiting for: "Let the fire fall!"

At that moment, the people on the cliff would push the glowing embers off and a spectacular fall of light would cascade down the cliff, accompanied by the oohs and aahs of the multitude below. The embers landed on ledges and caused no additional fires.

It was also a signal for thieves in the parking area to break into unattended cars, drivers to stop in the middle of the road and jump out for a photograph amidst a cacophony of honking horns, and 2,000 or so Instamatic camera flashbulbs to go off during a ten-second period. On one evening, a motorcycle gang blocked the bridge on the main road and created a traffic jam of New York City proportions as they, too, watched the falling fire.

The mythology of the event was ingrained in the minds of people. I would always see an outlier group sitting on the logs below Yosemite Falls, far away from the event. These folks believed that they had seen the fire coming over the waterfall when they were children. You could not disabuse them of their belief, even though the firefall occurred on the opposite side of the valley. One goofy seasonal ranger with a sense of humor even put a plastic label under a switch behind the information desk and when he'd see the glow before the embers were about to be pushed, he'd step back, saying, "Time for the firefall!" and flip the dummy switch, much to the amazement of a few gullible tourists.

With park visitor numbers headed over the two-million mark, the National Park Service decided the Firefall was an artificial, unnecessary attraction and stopped allowing it. Those of us on the front line heard complaints about the cancellation in a hurry. The outrage was immediate as generations of people who had seen the spectacle during their childhoods and were bringing their children and grandchildren to see it had to settle for the waterfalls. My own children sat on the stoop behind our house wearing long faces as they watched the final Firefall.

So many park visitors wrote complaints to the superintendent about canceling the Firefall event that for a time, each ranger was given a bundle of letters every day and we were required to write personal replies to every letter. Some of the incoming letters were quite abusive, and we learned to write bland and friendly replies to people who referred to us as hidden parts of human anatomy.

The Wawona Tunnel Tree

There may be no better example of the changes in values associated with the first century of the National Park Service than the saga of the Wawona Tunnel Tree, a famous giant sequoia that stood in Mariposa Grove until 1969. At the time I first saw it, the tree was believed to have been between fifty and a hundred years old when Christ was born. The giant sequoia was 234 feet tall and 26 feet in diameter. It was a major attraction by any measure. People drove across the country just to photograph their car and its occupants passing through the tree. If you talked to the park tour companies, it was a cash cow and as important as the spectacular scenery. Environmentalists looked at it as a work of official vandalism and an abomination.

Back in 1881, the Yosemite Stage and Turnpike Co. was supposed to have paid two brothers, the Scribners, $75 to cut the tunnel through an area of the tree that had been previously damaged by fire. The resultant tunnel was big enough to drive stagecoaches carrying tourists through. And over the following eighty-eight years it served its purpose well. There is no official count of the number of cars that have driven through the tree over the years, but it has to be substantial. Year after year, cars lined up and paused for snapshots, and rangers kept the traffic flowing and the disputes at a minimum. Early park leaders had allowed many such artificial attractions to be created and considered them a positive way to get people out to see their national treasures.

Fast forward to the winter of 1968–69. A plan was made to reduce the traffic jams by providing a shuttle to take visitors into the grove and through the tree tunnel. Shuttle tour vehicles were purchased and drivers were hired and trained. In the spring, the deep snow in the grove was attacked by the Park Service's snow plows and blowers, and all of the forces were marshaled to start a new era for one of the park's premium attractions.

But Mother Nature had other plans. She was still fuming about the damage done to one of her oldest creations, and during the winter she had sent in a big storm that blew the tree down. A snow plow driver was the first to see the fallen big tree and he came out to report his discovery.

To this day, visitors who saw the tunnel tree during its heyday still show up with their grandchildren and are disappointed. Some have even requested that another tree be cut open to provide future generations with the same experience. In fact, the opposite is taking place. The Park Service believes that road use in the grove has damaged the shallow rooting systems of the giant sequoias and they have closed the grove for a few years, during which the roads will be replaced by boardwalk trails and other facilities that will be more beneficial to these rare trees.

The remains of the tunnel tree are now marked with a sign that reads "Fallen Tunnel Tree." But here's an interesting kicker to the whole story. Like their cousins, the Sempervirens redwoods on the coast, these trees have a remarkable ability to reproduce from the fallen tree itself. If left alone, there could be new trees sprouting up from this giant, and in a couple of thousand years, who knows?

Nobody's Perfect

Everyone's entitled to a few mistakes, and I certainly am no exception. While working a wildfire burning on a steep slope above El Capitan, I got my crew to dig a fire line around the burn and we were "mopping up" and getting hot spots put out when I noticed that the lightning-struck tree, a tall red fir, had some smoke coming from an area on its crown a hundred-plus feet above. It would have to come down. We had plenty of room within the fire line to catch it so I cleared the crew out of the fall area and had the sawyer take the tree down.

The sawyer was accurate with his cut and the tree came down with a bang right where I wanted it—and then gravity took over. It started to slide. Down the slope it went, sounding like a runaway locomotive. I had nightmarish visions of it shooting off the cliff like a gigantic flaming arrow right down where the visitors were driving into the valley. Fortunately, it slowed and stopped. But the crew had to dig a fire line down the hill to contain it while we put the fire out.

On another fire, I dropped a tree on my backpack, which I hadn't stashed far enough away, and smashed the aluminum frame beyond recognition. While fighting a structure fire in one of the old wooden buildings at the Yosemite Lodge, I chopped a hole in the roof and prepared to shoot water from the nozzle of the fire hose into the attic where the fire was burning. Just as I opened the nozzle, the assistant chief ranger, wearing a fire fighter's white turnout coat and helmet, opened the hatch from below and was doused with water and a mess of ashes and charcoal. When he was helped down from his ladder, he looked like the coyote that gets blown up in the Road Runner cartoons. I was on his crap list for a while.

The enforcement duties were being shuffled onto my shoulders in increasing amounts. One evening I arrested a man for fighting and recognized him from my years as a deputy sheriff. I was doing the same job I had been doing for a lot less pay! But I wasn't unhappy. How could I be, working in one of the most beautiful places in the world? But I had visions of the back country and the wilderness.

CHAPTER 9

My Children Get Me to Alaska

On one midnight shift I was pinning up notices on the employee bulletin board when I came across an unusual one. The regional office in San Francisco was looking for a ranger with two or more elementary school children to transfer to Glacier Bay National Monument. The one-room Gustavus School for grades one through eight, where employees' children attended, was scheduled for closure by the State of Alaska if there were not sixteen students attending. My three would bring the number up to seventeen. For a ranger who wanted to go to a true wilderness, this was a golden opportunity.

I copied the notice, took it home, consulted my wife Susie, filled out an application, and mailed it the same morning. A week later I was called to the office and told I was being transferred to Alaska. We sold the car to another ranger, packed our few belongings, begged a ride to the airport in San Francisco and flew to Juneau.

North to Alaska

If you fly into Juneau on a commercial airliner today, you leave the aircraft on a Jetway and walk into a secured lounge with comfortable seats and exhibits of Alaskan history and wildlife. It's a nice little airport. Back in the 1960s, though, it was different.

It was raining when we got off the plane at the Juneau airport. It usually is. At the bottom of the steps there was a trail of wooden pallets leading to a door. We tiptoed across the pallets in order to avoid splashing into the deep puddles. One of the only other Hawai'ians in Juneau was the airport police officer on duty. He recognized me as Hawai'ian and we greeted each other. When he learned about my new assignment, he insisted on lending me his car to shuttle my family and luggage to our hotel. The kinship of Hawai'ians can be found in some unusual places.

We spent a couple of days in Juneau outfitting the kids and ourselves with wool jackets, rain gear, and rubber boots. Doris Howe, Superintendent Bob Howe's wife, took us around and introduced us to the manager of the Foodland grocery store. Park employees got groceries shipped to them on the park boat every eight weeks. We filled out sheets of paper with the things we would buy if we were shopping in person, and the employees would do their best to package up eight weeks' worth of groceries from our lists and occasionally toss in something they thought we might like. The store would send a bill along with the groceries and we'd send a check back with the boat skipper. It was the honor system. Nobody was using credit cards out in the bush and if you didn't do the honorable thing and pay up, you didn't get any more groceries.

There was a similar visit to the state library in Juneau. We wrote down the things our family was interested in reading, and once each month, the mail plane would come out carrying twenty-five books for us. We'd read them and send them back on the next month's airplane visit. We could also request books and the library was extremely good at finding them and getting them to us. My kids became avid readers and remain so to this day.

After the library, we visited the Park Service office where all the paperwork had been done by June Branner, the park administrative assistant. We were then driven back to the Juneau airport, boarded a Grumman Goose amphibious seaplane from Alaska Coastal-Ellis Air, and headed for Glacier Bay.

A half hour or so later, the Goose set down in Bartlett Cove. The pilot lowered his wheels into the water and ran us up onto the beach in front of the Glacier Bay Lodge. He climbed up a stepladder and unloaded our luggage from the trunk in the nose of the aircraft, tossing it all down to me. Then he buttoned the whole rig up, taxied around on the beach, ran back into the water, pulled the wheels up, idled out to an opening, and with a loud roar from the big radial engines, lifted off for his return trip.

My family was put up in a mobile home for a few weeks and then moved to a house that had the greatest view of any house I've ever been in. On clear days we could see Mount Fairweather and many of the other peaks in the Saint Elias Range. On occasion, humpback and minke whales and orcas could be seen out the living room window as they cruised through Bartlett Cove. Bald eagles were regular visitors, as were many other birds. The Coast Guard buoy tender ship brought out the old Peugeot station wagon we'd purchased in Juneau and set it on the dock.

The rangers at Yosemite had given me a copy of *Glacier Bay: The Land and the Silence*, the large-format Sierra Club publication written and photographed by Dave Bohn. I have read all of the books in the Sierra Club large-format series, and I'm convinced that Dave Bohn's book is the best. Many coffee table–sized books are long on graphics and short on writing. Dave's *Glacier Bay* is not only a beautiful book filled with breathtaking black and white photographs, but his treatment of the history and cultural connections of the place are well researched and sensitively written. My copy of the book sits in my Alaska cabin and is well thumbed by visitors.

CHAPTER 10

Glacier Bay National Monument

National monument? Isn't that manmade, like the Washington Monument or the Statue of Liberty? Here was one of the world's premier natural reserves, bigger even than Yellowstone National Park. What's the difference? Here's the easy answer. National parks are set aside by a Congressional action. A national monument may be set aside by Presidential proclamation. In 1925, President Calvin Coolidge made the Glacier Bay area into a national monument because of the uniqueness of the glacial retreat and the value of the place as an ecological study area. The monument was later enlarged and is now, together with its adjacent Canadian neighbor, one of the largest nature preserves in the world.

My new station at Bartlett Cove was positioned a few miles in from the mouth of the bay. A glacier had covered the entrance to the bay when it was observed and recorded by Captain George Vancouver in 1794. Tlingit tradition has the glaciers coming down from the north and chasing the people out of their homeland. The descendants of those people now reside across the waters in Hoonah. In 1968, the glaciers had receded sixty-five miles from where Captain Vancouver observed the ice and were now well up in the fjords, some right on the US–Canada border. To patrol this 4,000-plus square mile park we had a 26-foot Bertram twin-engine boat and a Uniflite 16-foot runabout that looked like its designer was in love with a 1957 Plymouth. It actually had fins and carried a big V4 outboard on the stern. These were, respectively, the best and the worst boats available at the time.

Chief Ranger Chuck Janda was a boating expert and I was a novice. My boating experience was limited to when I was a boy running a plywood sea skiff to go fishing out of Santa Cruz with a five-horse outboard my uncle lent me. On my first day on the job, Chuck handed me a copy of *Chapman's Manual on Seamanship and Small Boat Handling* and told me to read the first chapter. He told me I would not be allowed to run either boat until he was satisfied that I knew the ropes.

Each night I would read a chapter and on the following day Chuck would talk with me about the subject matter. I learned practical boat handling as the passenger ranger on long patrols of 100 miles and more. The tides in Glacier Bay have as much as 24 feet of vertical drop on their biggest day, and the currents and tide rips are substantial. Add to that the icebergs and winter sheet ice, and I couldn't have found a better place to learn to handle a small craft in difficult conditions than Glacier Bay.

One thing I learned was that minor repairs could shut down operations quickly. Parts were a long distance away and we were the only emergency crew stationed anywhere nearby. So the chief ranger had us down scrubbing the motor compartment and changing oil and other maintenance duties on a regular basis. We rangers exaggerated, saying that Chuck had us go over the engine with Q-tips, but it wasn't much of an exaggeration.

It didn't take long for the serious work to begin. On July Fourth of 1968 the small community was gathered on the beach near the housing area for a picnic when the Coast Guard called. The MV *Seacrest*, the park concessioner's tour boat, had struck something that had poked a hole in the hull and the captain had transmitted a mayday message. The Coast Guard was 130 miles away and we were it.

We got the park patrol boat out of its mooring and made haste to the location of the accident. After an hour and a half run we found the 65-footer with its bow on the beach at Wolf Cove in Muir Inlet. The passengers had been put ashore, and the bilge pumps were going full blast. Full blast wasn't sufficient, so the deck hand Greg Howe and two young army doctors, who were on vacation, were standing down in the bilges with buckets and five-gallon cans scooping water and handing it up through the hatch to the captain who was pouring it overboard. I was next in the bailing department, so I jumped down into the water and took over with another ranger to spell the exhausted men.

The chief ranger figured we wouldn't be enough to keep the boat afloat, so he ran the patrol boat back to Bartlett Cove, and in three more hours he was back with a portable fire pump. We had been taking turns bailing during his absence and were mighty glad when the suction hose came snaking down through the hatch. We got the pump going and got the water out of the bilges. The captain carved a plug to fit the hole, wrapped a T-shirt around it, and hammered the big plug into the hole. Then we loaded passengers back on, put some of them in the patrol boat, and slowly made our way back, getting in around four a.m.

In 1968 Glacier Bay National Monument probably received fewer than 4,000 visitors. Most flew in on seaplanes that would land them on the float at Bartlett Cove early in the morning. The visitors would walk across to the tour boat, a 65-foot long wooden World War II US Navy relic captained by Howard Robinson, a cranky and colorful character. Robby would take the boat on a 130-mile round trip to the Muir Glacier. People would see whales, colonies of seabirds and, if lucky, the calving of icebergs that sloughed off from the great glacier with a roar and an enormous splash.

Each day a ranger would travel on the boat, lecture about the geology and history of the place, and answer questions about the puffins, eiders, and myriad other critters most people were seeing for the first time. Greg Streveler, my fellow park ranger, was the best at interpreting the park for the visitors. He was an accomplished biologist who knew more about the ecosystem of the place than any of us. Later, Bruce Paige came on board as the first park naturalist at Glacier Bay and he became an authority on the diverse bird fauna of southeast Alaska.

I was learning on the job. My assignment was to supervise a couple of seasonal rangers who worked the areas of Excursion Inlet and Dundas Bay, manage the fire control operations, do any law enforcement, manage the weather station, and fill in whenever needed on the tour boat.

The Park Service also sent me to Sitka for a two-week program to become an emergency medical technician. Being an EMT in Alaska is a little different. They taught us to do tracheotomies, wound stitching, and other serious treatments well beyond first aid. There was no doctor around except for Jack Lesh, a remarkable man who left his practice and together with his wife Sally, had taken over the operation of the Gustavus Inn. In extreme emergencies Jack would help, but otherwise, I was it. During my career I have delivered two babies, stitched wounds, splinted broken limbs, and applied lots of bandages to crying children.

One winter day we were transfixed with an event being transmitted over our single-side band radio. A Public Health Service surgeon at the hospital in Sitka was on the radio, instructing a Native Alaskan EMT. He was performing an appendectomy on a patient in a weathered-in village well north of us. The calm voice of the surgeon would say something like, "Now cut into the area where you've drawn the line. Don't be concerned with the surface blood, just don't go any deeper than the white tissue layer." We were transfixed as we heard all the instructions carried out with the EMT answering "Yah" or "No" and little else.

Evidently the remote control surgery was a success. I hoped I would never have to perform such a task.

In bad weather there is no evacuation possible. The children were trained pretty well to avoid injuries, but the opportunities for adventure are greater in Alaska than just about anywhere in North America, and the kids took advantage of those opportunities. We were lucky and the kids and adults got along without anything major happening. One of the biggest search efforts in Alaska occurred when the wife of one of the rangers who preceded me disappeared, prompting a massive search of the wild territory around Bartlett Cove. No trace has been found during the past fifty years and her fate is still a mystery.

CHAPTER 11

Science for the Long Haul

Climate is changing, there is no argument about that. But there is a big scrap about what's causing it. The argument is the equivalent of that old saw about rearranging the deck chairs on the *Titanic*. One way or another, the climate is changing. Arctic people in our own country are losing their villages as the ice pack disappears and the sea level rises and we are having a stupid argument about whether it exists and why. If it happens in New York, San Francisco, and New Orleans (again), we *might* change our behaviors. If we can moderate the natural component of this change by modifying what we do, perhaps we can slow the change to give time for adapting to the rising waters by redesigning the places we live. One of the reasons Glacier Bay was set aside ninety-four years ago was for the study of climate change.

The snow piles up in the Saint Elias Range above Glacier Bay. It pushes downhill, causing big rivers of ice to fill the valleys and fjords and push icebergs off into the sea. The faces of these glaciers rise up to 300 feet above the surface and some are all the way to the bottom as the ice breaks off. These Alaskan glaciers have surged forward in the past, and according to the

Tlingit people, the ice started backing up somewhere around the time the first Europeans spotted them. Unlike anywhere else in the world, the glaciers in this bay have been headed back to their origins at an accelerated rate. What can we learn from this phenomenon?

Enter science. In 1922, William Cooper, a professor of ecology at the University of Minnesota, began a lifelong study of the return of life to the scraped-over earth emerging as the glaciers backed up. Barren areas he identified in his studies are now covered in forests. The chronology of the plants and animals that colonize the new earth, observed and measured over the past, give us a picture of what happened in North America as the last ice age retreated to the north. The research is invaluable.

As a student in the early 1920s, William O. Field became interested in the rapid retreat of the glaciers and began photographing them. In 1936 he began a systematic recording of the retreat of Glacier Bay's glaciers, which continues to this day. His measurements showed how quickly the change was taking place. From the time he began measuring until the present, the terminus of the Muir Glacier has retreated more than seven miles. I was fortunate to be assigned to carry Bill Field's equipment on one of his trips and learned about glaciers from a world-class geologist. Some glaciers I climbed during the 1960s are completely gone. Others have backed up from the water and are now dumping their terminal load onto the land.

Today there is a boom in climate research and other studies at Glacier Bay. The US Geological Survey has a study crew on site. Dr. Cooper and Dr. Field were pioneers and their work continues, even though they have both passed away.

CHAPTER 12

The Bull Moose Incident

On Pleasant Island, just across Icy Passage from the town of Gustavus, Alaska, is a place called Bull Moose Cove. Many visitors believe it to be named after the male moose, but it is not. On July 20, 1969, the fishing vessel *Bull Moose*, a 47-foot purse seiner, went down at Ancon Rock at the mouth of Glacier Bay. Crew members David Burns, of California, and Monte Boden, of Seattle, were trapped in the forecastle and lost their lives. One crew member swam down and pulled his brother out of the galley while the boat was sinking. Altogether four of the crew survived while hanging onto the net floats that had surfaced and remained attached to the boat.

Frank and Sally Kearns, the managers of the Glacier Bay Lodge, happened to be fishing out of their small Starcraft aluminum cruiser when they heard noises that sounded like seabirds calling. They could see some movement on the mass of floats that appeared to be floating kelp. But something caused Frank to motor over to investigate. He found the four men in the icy-cold water. He and Sally pulled them into their boat, radioed the ranger station, and headed back to Bartlett Cove.

I called Jack Lesh and got advice on what to do. My wife Susie drew a bath with water right around 104 degrees Fahrenheit and I took sleeping bags down to the float. When the boat arrived, we stuck each man into a sleeping bag that had been warmed by the truck heater and raced up to the house. Three of the men were shivering badly but had good vital signs. The fourth was below the shiver level and when I checked him, his body temperature was in the high 80-degree zone. We put him in the bath water, Jack Lesh gave him some kind of injection, and we fed him spoonfuls of warm chicken broth to get his body mass to warm up. The others stayed in the sleeping bags, drank soup, and did just fine. But it took a long time to get the fourth man back up to an adequate body temperature without having him go into shock.

On the following day we met the USCG *Sweetbrier*, a buoy tender, at the sinking site and helped raise the boat from the bottom and recover the bodies of the two fishermen. The boat was dragged over to Pleasant Island and left on the bottom of a tidal bay that is now known as Bull Moose Cove.

There is a lot of speculation over why the boat sank. Did it strike a rock? It could have been a big tide rip; in the past I have seen a ten-foot standing wave at the very place. To this day, it's still not determined. My own guess—and it is a guess—is that the boat was overpowered. It was originally powered by a slow-turning diesel engine, and had been repowered with a high-speed diesel. It carried a heavy seine skiff lashed on the rear deck. Time is money in the seine fishery where a single set can bring a big payday, so the days of rowing a skiff around the fish are over and speed is of the essence. All that weight and power added to whatever caused the boat to bury its bow, driving the *Bull Moose* right down into the water. An open hatch took on water and the forces of physics took over. The skipper told me that when the boat heeled at an extreme angle, he slipped on the flying bridge and may have hit the throttle as he fell, causing everything to speed up.

Regardless of the cause, each time I pass the cove, the sad story of what happened to the two fishermen reminds me of the power of the elements, and the need to take care.

Sitakaday Narrows

There was no coast and geodetic survey chart of the waters of Glacier Bay at the time I served there. Chief Ranger Janda had located and noted many hazards by running a recording depth sounder on the park patrol boat, but there were still a lot of unknowns. The hazard that was most familiar was Sitakaday Narrows. Three miles wide and much shallower than the upper parts of Glacier Bay, the narrow channel forced all of the upper bay waters into a slot. On a tidal change of 25 vertical feet, the waters contained in three major fjords and many smaller ones came pouring down, flowed over reefs and around islands and caused rips and whirls that made navigation exciting.

While making a passage through the narrows against the tidal current, boaters sometimes were pressing against a current that exceeded eight knots. The park tour boat would often heel one way and then the other as the water swirled back and forth. I once experienced a stiff wind from the south meeting a big outgoing tide and pushing up a steep wave, perhaps six feet high. I had to turn and run before it, shelter behind an island, and wait out the tide change before I could proceed through.

There was another side to this phenomenal place; it was a feeding site for big and small creatures of land and sea. On the east side of the narrows was the Beardslee Entrance, where boaters could go into protected waters among dozens of little islands. At the interface with the fast narrows current was a biological soup made up of the tiniest plankton on up to some of the world's largest mammals. Humpback whales, Stellar sea lions, and hair seals frequent the place along with harbor porpoises, and in recent years, dozens of sea otters. While fishing there I hooked and released a halibut that may have weighed 300 pounds. I once watched a brown bear feeding on a fresh whale carcass washed up on the beach and I saw an eight- or nine-foot long salmon shark swim beneath my skiff. Pods of orcas passed by and had a look at the orca totems painted on my boat's hull. I have caught many salmon and halibut along that stretch over the years.

In 1984, well after my service at Glacier Bay, my fiancée Narda Pierce and I were kayaking back from a 100-mile round trip voyage when we encountered another side of this place. At the Beardslee Entrance we were paddling on what appeared to be calm water. But we could hear what sounded like a waterfall and when I glanced at the shore, I noticed that the calm water was carrying us along at a fast clip. We were headed for a small standing wave line about ten inches high. I steered the kayak to cross the wave at a right angle, but when we hit it, the water we were traveling on shot under the wave and it caught us and torqued the boat over into a capsize.

I got myself out and surfaced next to the boat with my paddle in hand but I couldn't see Narda. Her paddle was floating west and she had surfaced under the cockpit and soon emerged. We had practiced with this Klepper boat in warmer waters, and I handed my paddle to Narda, climbed onto the hull, and righted it. I crawled up from the stern, bailed as much water as I could, and pulled her in. We chased down her paddle and headed for the shore of Young Island, a mile or so away.

I had some body fat but Narda was pretty fit and was going hypothermic in a hurry. These glacier-fed waters are very cold. We were wearing wool and had no wet or dry suits on. At the shore I set the tent up, got her out of her clothes and into a sleeping bag while I fired up the stove and heated a lifesaving Lipton's Cup-a-Soup to get her going. After she stopped shivering, we got some of her dry clothes out of the waterproof bags, packed the boat, and headed for Bartlett Cove. Around the island we came upon a charter fishing boat from the park lodge, and when the guide saw the condition we were in, he poured us hot tea in paper cups and handed them out the port window of his boat, almost like a floating Starbucks driveup. I've never had a more warming drink. We paddled the last five or so miles back to the lodge, squished our way into the dining room in wet rubber boots and clothing and ordered cheeseburgers and hot fudge sundaes in celebration of our survival.

The following year I learned that Bob Howe was taking bets in Gustavus on whether they would ever see Narda again after that experience. We fooled him and got married the following year and have paddled through the area many times since. But never on a big tide change.

Bob Howe

Glacier Bay's Park Superintendent Robert Howe was a ranger's ranger. He was old school and believed that a superintendent's job was out in the park. Bob's office was in Juneau, sixty-five miles away by boat or airplane. He left the office duties to an administrative officer and a secretary and spent a lot of time in the park boating, hiking, and talking with visitors about their experiences. He wanted to experience as much of wild Alaska as he could. Chuck Janda, the chief ranger, and the rest of the employees were pretty good at their jobs so Bob exercised his supervisory responsibilities by bugging us all to get out in the park and away from our desk. Yes, that was singular. We had only one desk for the four of us so it wasn't hard to follow his advice.

A ranger friend told me that Bob had been the park biologist at Yellowstone during the contentious debates about burgeoning elk populations and the lack of wolves and what to do about it. During one particular nasty public hearing in Missoula, a rancher in the audience apparently called Bob a liar. The story goes that Bob took off his uniform jacket, jumped into the audience, and promptly punched the rancher. After he was pulled off, I heard that more ranchers were willing to talk with him. They either respected his toughness or thought the guy he punched was a jerk.

Bob had us out on snowshoes packing through wilderness passes no one in recent memory had been through. We snowshoed with him up onto glaciers in winter to check snow depths for long-range weather forecasting, and he once showed me how to pull up a heavy commercial crab pot from his canoe without tipping it over. On one occasion we accompanied him on the park supply boat, MV *Nunatak*, out into the ocean and up to Lituya Bay. On the way back from that trip, Bob and I were taking photographs and were nearly flushed off the foredeck of the boat as we went through the Lituya entrance, one of the worst crossings in the Pacific. All of the rangers except Bob, who was a Navy veteran, got seasick and vomited for hours on the way home.

And not surprisingly, rangers had boats for personal use. With no local store, we fished for our fresh food needs, and also used the boats for recreation, taking our families and friends around the waters of Icy Straits and Glacier Bay on weekends. Chuck Janda had a fiberglass runabout, Greg Streveler had a big wooden Banks Dory. I bought a boat called a Bartender, a double-ended planing hybrid that had a big outboard mounted inboard. Bob Howe owned a fiberglass cabin cruiser that got a lot of use taking visiting Park Service people fishing and on expeditions into the park. That boat, however, was destined for disaster.

On a gorgeous summer day, Bob and an old buddy of his from the Yellowstone days were headed out of Bartlett Cove to go fishing when the boat blew up. Roland "Gildy" Gildersleeve, the pilot who flew chartered flights and air tours in the park, was just lifting off in his Cessna float plane when right in front of and just below his plane, Bob's engine hatch cover came flying up in the air! Gildy radioed the ranger station and circled as Bob's boat began burning. He watched Bob and his buddy launch the little dinghy and escape as the fire started to burn hot and take over the whole boat. He told me that the two had no paddles and were furiously paddling with their hands, sometimes just spinning around as they escaped from the burning boat. By the time we arrived with the patrol boat, Bob's boat had burned to the waterline, and the remaining fiberglass was sinking. Of everything on his vessel, Bob had managed to save only his camera.

Casual maintenance was probably the cause of the fireworks. Bob's gas tank had been getting intrusions of water. His solution was to install a big truck filter in the gas line, and when the boat engine would sputter and fail, he'd unscrew the canister on the filter and pour out the water and sediment. After screwing the canister back on and hitting the starter, an electric fuel pump would refill the filter and put gasoline back into the system and start the engine. Evidently, when the motor quit just outside of Bartlett Cove, Bob unscrewed the canister and pitched the O-ring gasket overboard along with the water, When he put the filter back on, closed the hatch, and turned on the system, it pumped gasoline into the engine compartment and when he hit the starter, it went *boom*! Fortunately, the fastenings on the hatch cover were screwed into soft wood and the hatch cover blew skyward. Had it been fastened well, there might have been a much worse outcome.

After Bob retired, he and his wife Doris had a home built next to the Salmon River in Gustavus, and he spent a lot of time running his aluminum skiff back and forth to the Inian Islands near the western entrance to Icy Straits where his two boys lived and fished commercially. Every Friday evening, a crowd would come to Bob and Doris's house for whiskey and companionship. Even though Bob and Doris have passed away, the "Bob Howe Night" weekly whiskey drinking continues at someone else's house in the little town of Gustavus.

CHAPTER 13

The Law North of Icy Straits

Once more my law enforcement training came into use. The law north of Icy Straits? I was it. Then again, there was not much crime. I had to threaten the Glacier Bay Lodge manager with closure if he didn't follow the cleanliness rules in his kitchen, but it was a hollow threat. I had to chew out the manager's children for throwing things at bears. But every so often, the state would close the purse seine fishery for a day or two and twenty purse seine boats would have to tie up to the dock and the crews would head for the bar at the lodge. I would have to be there at closing time to clear the place out and make sure the tipsy fishermen got back on the first boat tied up at the end of the dock. From there they would have to climb from boat to boat until they found theirs and could sleep off the booze.

I carried no firearm, and once in a while one of the crew members would have a little fun and overstep their bounds. I could usually use humor and firmness to get them back to their boat, but figured that someday I'd probably have to get physical. I started carrying a WW II Navy billy club my father brought back from the war. (I never asked him how he had acquired it.) It hung from a ring attached to my belt. When a drunk would challenge me I'd draw the club out of its carrier and ask if they had health insurance. Their buddies who were always there to watch the fun would suddenly come to their senses and drag away the belligerent drunk. Fortunately, I never had to use the club and it hangs inside my Alaska cabin shed for use in the event a bear sticks his head in the window.

One evening, I loaded some inebriated fishermen into the bed of the park pickup and drove them to their boats. After everyone was safely aboard, I went home. Later that night, a black bear, smelling a fresh fish that had been laid out on a bed of ice in a tub on the deck of the fourth boat, navigated his way to the fish and ate it. Then the bear explored the rest of the boat. The atmosphere was stuffy inside the forecastle of the purse seiner, so the crew had stuck a fifteen-inch piece of a two-by-four under one end of the hatch to hold it up in order to get some fresh air. In the bunks beneath the hatch four fishermen were asleep.

The bear stuck his head into the open end of the hatch and stared at a young drunk fisherman asleep in the top bunk a couple of feet below. Surprised to see the man, the bear huffed once, blowing the smell of undigested chum salmon into the fisherman's face. The fisherman got a rude awakening when he opened his eyes and saw their visitor and screamed, which followed by an equally surprised bellow by the bear. The bear raised up, knocked the prop out from the end of the hatch and was pinned by the neck as the hatch came down — and then all hell broke loose.

In addition to being curious animals, bears are incredibly strong. With a big lurch, the bear lifted the hatch by doing some kind of hairy pushup and hastily backed out, leaving the four groggy fishermen scrambling around in the dark. The ruckus was reported to my home phone by the baker at the lodge and I went to the dock to find a babbling fisherman surrounded by others who had not yet reached the hangover stage and were still pretty drunk. One of the fellows looked like he had seen something worse than a ghost and may have considered swearing off alcohol.

On another day, Alaska state troopers called us for assistance. There was a report of a drunk or deranged fisherman in a troller speeding around in the troll fleet off of Lemesurier Island, waving a 30-30 rifle and firing it in the air. Periodically, he would disappear and the boat would run itself in a big circle, causing the other fishing boats to get out of the way. Then he'd reappear and shoot off another round and yell something unintelligible at everyone. The troopers had no boat in the area and the Coast Guard was hours away, so they asked for our help.

A trooper was flown out on the patrol's De Havilland Beaver float plane, and Chief Ranger Janda and I met him with our patrol boat in the middle of Icy Straits. After we got the trooper aboard, we hung out until the fisherman made one of his periodic disappearances and I brought our boat alongside. The trooper glanced in, saw the drunk sprawled on the deck of his wheelhouse, and quickly climbed aboard the fishing boat and handcuffed him. We transferred the trooper and his catch back to a float plane, tied the troller behind our patrol boat and towed it back to Bartlett Cove. We anchored it in the headquarters lagoon and kept it until the fisherman made bail and came back to retrieve his vessel. In those days, the Alaska state troopers were like the Canadian Mounties. Why send out two when you only need one?

Life at a Remote Station

Susie and the children took to the Alaskan life. Nine miles away on a gravel road was the community of Gustavus. About 100 people lived in the place year around, and the population exploded to 250 or so in the summer when schoolteachers with homesteads and commercial fishermen with cabins returned. They were joined by a cohort of young people who pioneered the whole-earth movement of the 1970s and who came to build cabins, start gardens, and live close to the land. During summer, seasonal park and hotel employees added to the numbers. Not many homesteaders made a living off the land, and not many of the young people prospered from the short growing season, but they took what work was available, and together with the families of early pioneers and the few park employees they formed a community.

Eugene Chase, the Gustavus postmaster, was also a homesteader. Gene was a very kind man. Because we were not able to garden in the park, Gene would offer up a big area of his homestead and during the short growing season, park families were able to grow big gardens of potatoes, turnips, and other root vegetables. The irrigation system consisted of carrying buckets of water from a nearby drainage ditch and pouring the water on rows of plants during dry spells. The families of park employees who took advantage of Gene's largess didn't need gym memberships to grow strong and fit. With homegrown vegetables, fresh fish, and game meat, we lived a healthy life.

Back then there was no television available and the Juneau radio stations were too low-powered to reach us at night. We had an old Hallicrafters multi-band radio and at night we could tune in to Radio Moscow and listen to performances of classical music interspersed with cold-war propaganda. With a couple of beers, we could run our own versions of the propaganda and amuse ourselves with our own version of *Mystery Science Theater*. When the ionosphere was at the right altitude during the winter, we could tune in to KNBR from San Francisco and hear the news from the Lower 48 and Warriors basketball.

During winter the employees at the airfield in Gustavus would receive films for their recreation and would invite all of us to drive over and watch a B movie. We'd sit in a stuffy room on a few folding chairs while the kids sprawled on the floor to watch westerns. It seemed like whoever picked the films was a fan of the spaghetti westerns of that era. So we watched Italians playing Mexican bandits with English dubbed poorly onto the sound tracks. Audience comments were often much more entertaining than the film dialogue.

The other source of entertainment during long winters was the same as it is anywhere: music. Before joining the National Park Service I had purchased an old Harmony guitar for $15 at a pawn shop on South First Street in San Jose. The instrument became known as "the finger butcher" because of its high action. But despite the many wounds it inflicted on me, I taught myself to play using a book of songs by the Weavers and a paperback book of folk song lyrics. Jim Bob Hepburn, Glacier Bay's excellent mechanic, was also an excellent guitarist and we would have snacks and play music while our families sang. Fred Rose, an employee of the State of Alaska, had purchased a Wurlitzer organ, and we'd play guitar along with his boys John and Bob, who'd bang away on that organ. One day I was walking alongside some old buildings at the airfield and heard some classical music coming from near the water treatment facility at Gustavus. It turned out to be a talented young woman named Bonnie Harris, who had found a place that was heated year round and had her piano shipped out from Juneau. The Alaska bush is not the cultural wasteland you might believe from watching today's reality TV.

Our groceries came every eight weeks on the MV *Nunatak*. The boat was a 72-foot wooden vessel built for the US Biological Survey in the 1920s and had been used in the Bering Sea. She would do ten knots, and only ten knots, no matter if you had her at half or full throttle, and was an excellent boat for a base of field operations. Captain Jim Sanders was a former Coast Guard noncommissioned officer and knew his vessel and the waters very well. There was a cook-deckhand named Bill Meyers who was a backup at the helm, kept the boat reasonably well tidied up, and cooked our meals for us. Bill drank whiskey and read philosophy books in the evening and could be counted on for fascinating and hilarious discussions about politics and world events.

The downside to the old boat was that it was infested with cockroaches. Every eight weeks, when we toted our groceries from the boat to our houses, we would unload the boxes outside and after inspecting every package, take the groceries inside. We burned the boxes because the roaches would lay eggs in the corrugations of the cardboard and stow away into our pantries.

On a trip to Muir Inlet, our regional director was aboard and Bill Meyers had purchased steaks for all of us. As he served the hot platters with steaks and potatoes, a roach dropped off the overhead and landed on the regional director's steak. He jumped up and yelled at Bob Howe, "Howe, why don't you get rid of these goddamned cockroaches!" Seizing the opportunity, Bob grabbed his briefcase and pulled out a sheaf of old requests for funding for that exact purpose and told him, "I've been asking for this for three years and you keep turning me down!"

With a lot of cursing, the regional director said he was no longer hungry and retired to his bunk. Ranger Greg Streveler and I cut out a little piece of the steak the roach had landed on and split the rest between us.

But Bill Meyers, the cook, had the last word. He looked at us and said, "I saw that bugger walking across the overhead and just as he got to the right place I willed him. Under my breath I said, 'Drop, you sonofabitch,' and he did."

That winter, the MV *Nunatak* was taken to Seattle for a haulout and finally fumigated. We had Bill and his trained roach to thank.

On weekends, we would fish for halibut and salmon and dig clams and cockles. During hunting season we'd go to islands outside the park to hunt for deer and ducks. I got to know George Dalton Sr., a Tlingit elder from the village of Hoonah. George was the best rod and reel fisherman I ever met. He knew where and when to fish and when to stay ashore. We always hoped the fishing would be good, but George Dalton actually knew. He also was good at calling deer. One of my friends, Skip Wallen, told me that George took him hunting on an island. When they got out on the beach George plucked a blade of rye grass, stretched it in his hands, and blew on it like a reed in a wind instrument. Deer came out of the woods and George told Skip, "Shoot that one for me." Then they moved to another location and he called more deer and he said, "Shoot that one for yourself."

During winter when fresh food was tough to get, the king crab boats would be working the deep waters nearby. It was a signal for local residents to start baking sourdough rye bread. The odors coming from the kitchen caused some drooling, but we were all shooed out until the loaves were finished. About the time the bread was scheduled to come out of the ovens, we'd radio the crab boats and ask if they needed bread. They always did, so we ran a boatload of fresh loaves out to them and would bring back several huge king crabs. A call would go out to the community at Gustavus and people would show up with side dishes and salads. In our shop we always had a clean barrel with a wooden lid. We'd fire up the steam cleaner, drop the nozzle through a hole in the lid and steam all the crabs. With a big heater going, and plywood sheets spread across saw horses, the annual crab/bread swap always ended up as one of winter's highlights.

Poisoned Clams

For a while we ate clams according to the adage "Eat clams and oysters only in months containing the letter 'R.' " Thus, don't eat clams during the period between May through August. Originally, when refrigeration wasn't available, that had to do with spoilage. But in the 1960s it had more to do with paralytic shellfish poisoning. This occurs when clams and other shellfish filter thousands of gallons of sea water through their systems and acquire concentrations of tiny dinoflagellates and other organisms. We had noticed some slight tingling and numbness from eating cockles, but didn't think much about it until I was visiting on the research vessel *Acona* that was operated by the University of Alaska. The scientists on board were testing surf clams for toxicity. They diluted a tiny bit of clam meat about 1,000 to one and, using an eyedropper, fed one drop to a lab mouse. Within a couple of seconds the mouse flipped over dead. We stopped eating the local shellfish and I have seen various accounts of the CIA using the poison as an assassination tool during the cold war. I have no idea if that's true, but we were all reading Ian Fleming's James Bond novels at the time and were willing to believe it.

Previous page: Big Basin State Park, 1923. Author's mother, seen here at age six, is with her parents on the left. *Photographer unknown – property of the author*

Boy Scouts backpacking in High Sierra wilderness, 1954

Sue Menger Cahill at the Grizzly Giant tree in Yosemite's Mariposa Grove, 1967

Upper Yosemite Falls, 1967

Author on the canyon wall with rescue litter at Grand Canyon National Park, 1966

Ranger patrol boat with photographer at Reid Glacier, Glacier Bay
National Monument, 1968. *Photo by Charles V. Janda*

Illegal commercial fishing operation at Lituya Bay, Glacier Bay National Monument, 1968. *Photo by Charles V. Janda*

Mt. Katmai collapsed caldera. Site of one of the largest eruptions during the 20th century. Katmai National Monument, 1969

Park technician Robert Kokubun in Haleakala National Park, 1972

The author examines a blooming ahinahina (silversword plant) in the Haleakala Crater. Haleakala National Park, 1973. *Photo by M. Woodbridge Williams*

Credits: Unless otherwise identified, all photos are by the author.

CHAPTER 14

Visiting Time

In the late 1960s, Alaska was like a gigantic small town. Some friends spent winters in the bush up on the Kobuk River, living in houses designed after native dwellings from early times. Others went home to their cabins, often up in the interior where deep cold was a constant companion and a wood supply wasn't just for decorative fires, but for survival. We kept track of one another, and, when adversity reared its head, people went to help. A circle of friends today might span a fair-size city limit in size. Our Alaskan circle of friends spread over a thousand or so miles.

One early winter day a small float plane landed in the cove. It was typical southeast Alaskan weather, with cold rain and mid-30 degrees Fahrenheit. The airplane float had been taken in for the season so the big storms wouldn't rip it off its moorings and we were not expecting company. The pilot secured his aircraft to the remaining dock float and was soon knocking on my door. When I answered, I saw a man of medium height standing there, soaking wet and shivering. He stuck out his hand and said, "Hi, I'm Ed Cahill. I heard there was another Cahill here, so I thought I'd drop in." After we got him tea and something to eat, we had a good chat. He turned out to be an engineer employed by the State of Alaska and had flown out from Juneau out of pure curiosity. We became friends and have crossed paths many times since that visit. But the memory of that knock on the door remains with me. I learned that no one in a remote place is truly independent. In Alaska your neighbors may be a long distance from you in miles, but they are close when you need them.

One September day, as the summer season was closing down, a large yacht cruised into Bartlett Cove and anchored up. It was the *Wild Goose*, a converted minesweeper owned by the actor John Wayne. I motored a skiff out to the boat and found two of the crew in a Boston Whaler working on an outboard motor that needed some repair. Their boat was bouncing around, so I invited them to bring the motor into our shop and work on it there. They were happy to do so and were able to get the thing repaired and back to the yacht that evening. The next day, John Wayne himself came to the ranger office to thank us. He also asked about a pilot for going up to the glaciers with his vessel. When he found out that Chief Ranger Janda was the one who knew the waters best, he offered a bargain. If Chuck would act as pilot, Mr. Wayne would invite all of the children in Gustavus to accompany him and his son for the day trip. Calls went out, and eight or ten children showed up and got a trip on the big boat. They came home with autographs and stories of the lunches served to them in the dining area. My children were most impressed with the fresh apples they were given to bring home.

Mining and Choppers

During Franklin Roosevelt's presidency, homesteaders and miners and some of their influential friends lobbied in Washington, DC, to exclude Gustavus from the boundaries of the national monument. Mining was allowed to continue within the boundaries of the monument, and during my assignment at Glacier Bay, I had to visit many of the mining sites to make certain the operating rules and agreements were being followed. Bert Parker's mine on Ptarmigan Creek was an old-fashioned Alaska mine site. When the mine was active, Bert and some of the Parker family would work the prospect during summer. Other operations at Muir Inlet and beach-placer prospects south of Cape Fairweather on the coast had to be checked as well.

The most remarkable operation was being run by Newmont Mining atop the Brady Glacier. The Brady is a huge piedmont glacier that is fed by massive amounts of snowfall in the St. Elias Range. It feeds glaciers that move north, south, and east, spilling ice into Glacier Bay and Icy Straits. The miners were housed in wall tents perched on the moving glacier ice, and they had flexible drill rigs boring through hundreds of feet of slowly moving ice to bring up core samples of the rich mineral deposits beneath the ice. Their plan was to build a port on the coast at Dixon Harbor and bore a tunnel under the glacier to extract the ore.

Chief Ranger Janda and I helicoptered up to the site to check on their compliance as Newmont was shutting down for the season. With the differences in air density over sunwarmed forest areas and glacier ice, it was a bumpy ride. At the drill site we met two Austrian alpinists who had been hired to keep the miners safe. Each day they would take long probes and poke them through the snow to find where there might be crevasses developing and they would plot and flag work areas so the miners didn't fall through.

What I observed that day was the most bizarre work site I could ever have imagined. We were told that on a previous day, the alpinists had opened the door on their wall tent and during the previous night a crevasse had opened up just outside their temporary dwelling. We did our inspection and flew back down to Dundas Bay to meet our boat. My dislike of helicopter travel was reinforced the following week when the helicopter we had flown in was blown from the sky by a poorly timed exploration blast at another prospect outside the park. Lives were lost.

During that same year we also participated in a search for a missing helicopter in the eastern part of the park. A Juneau helicopter pilot had taken some hunters to a ridge in the mountains near Excursion Inlet. It was illegal to hunt immediately after landing. The rule was made to avoid the unfair advantage of spotting from the air and landing near trophy mountain goats and sheep. What appeared to have been an illegal hunt was cut short when the pilot walked uphill while the rotors were moving and was decapitated by his own ship. The hunters could not figure out how to operate the radio, so they waited until they were spotted by search planes and, together with their companion's gruesome remains, were airlifted out.

Today, the national monument has become a national park and all mining operations have been terminated. There are still some legal issues floating around but no one is drilling on the Brady Glacier any more.

Wildlife

There were a lot of black bears around the lower parts of Glacier Bay. I once observed two dozen or so grazing and foraging in one big area between Point Carolus and Dundas Bay. Some of the bear activities were humorous. One ranger purchased a tetherball device for his children, but a black bear that found it had its own fun. The bear grabbed the ball in his jaws and pulled it until it released from his mouth and flew to the end of the tether. The bear, obviously having enjoyed it, jumped around a little until he or she could get the ball again. After a couple of turns, however, the ball popped, startling the bear, which backed away. That bear was a playful one, since later on it found the inflated rubber raft I used as a dinghy in my skiff, popped that too and ripped it into shreds.

On a patrol to Reid Inlet with two other rangers, we anchored the park patrol boat in a safe place and left our plastic Sport-Yak dinghy high on the beach. After hiking to the face of Reid Glacier, we came back to find the dinghy with holes in its outer hull. A glance told us that it had to have been a very large Alaska brown bear to get a bite that big. Not only that, the bear had taken more than one bite. After some serious looking around to make sure the bear was gone, we drew straws to determine who the lucky guy would be to paddle out to get the boat. I lost.

As I paddled out into the icy water, I could hear two things. One, air was blasting out of the bite holes above the water as the hull filled with water, and two, the two guys on the beach were having hysterics. After I had gotten the anchor up and finally motored in to pick them up, they told me why they had been laughing. The dinghy had two very short oars and they said I was rowing and splashing so much water with the little oars that it looked like a Mixmaster flying through the water!

A few weeks later at the Glacier Bay Lodge, a young male black bear cornered Maude, the lodge manager's mother-in law, in the supply room and had gotten into the food supplies while she took refuge on top of stacks of boxes of groceries. The bear left, but a day later it showed up at my house and tried to break into the house through a window. I had to shoot the bear. It turned out that lodge employees had been feeding scraps to the bear and one had shot blunted arrows at him and harassed him for their own amusement. Like the Yosemite bears, this one had been doomed by people feeding him.

Now, nearly fifty years later, moose may occasionally be seen just below the rooms at the Glacier Bay Lodge, and brown bears have arrived at the town of Gustavus. An infestation of spruce bark beetles in the 1980s caused a major die-off of trees in the areas around Bartlett Cove. The openings caused by the loss of these trees are being filled by alder trees, which fix nitrogen in the soils, and hemlock trees that have replaced the spruce trees over time. It has turned into a great place to study what happens under natural conditions, but in an accelerated course of time.

Sea Otters

In 1969 we were asked to participate in the plan to relocate sea otters from Amchitka Island to Southeast Alaska's coast. Sea otters had been missing from the coast since they were extirpated by Russian and American fur traders in the 1800s. The federal government was preparing to test nuclear devices far to the north under Amchitka Island, and either from fear of the damage to the otters or for its pure public relations value they decided to fund the transfer of several sea otters to their former homes in Southeast. We stood by at Gustavus Airfield with Grumman Goose seaplanes, and waited for the otters' arrival.

Alaska Airlines cargo liners landed and discharged a couple of dozen sea otters in secured cages out onto the airfield. We picked them up and loaded them into the Grummans and put a couple of rangers on each aircraft. The planes flew to small bays on the open ocean and rangers horsed the cages into the open hatch and dumped the otters into the water. In one aircraft, an overanxious ranger unlocked a cage while his partner was discharging the otter in another cage. The rear end of the ranger who was leaning out the hatch got the only sea otter bite any of us knew of.

After the otters hit the water they hauled out on the rocks and groomed themselves, probably getting rid of the odors of the people who had handled them, and then swam off to the kelp beds. Some of the otter transplants didn't work, but later ones were successful, and today, a large population of sea otters exists well up into Glacier Bay. Coincidentally, the Dungeness crab population has dwindled to very low levels and the otters are being blamed.

Today, nearly five decades after I served at the park, lower Glacier Bay is different. Icebergs are less in evidence in the lower bay as the glaciers continue to recede. There is much more species diversity in the forest and moose have moved into the area. Wolves and brown bears have appeared and coyotes are rarely seen.

CHAPTER 15

Lituya Bay

No discussion of my time at Glacier Bay would be complete without a visit to Lituya Bay. The ill-fated expedition of Count La Perouse stopped there to measure astronomical events in July 1786. Several officers and men were lost in what is certainly the worst bay entrance on the coast of Alaska. It is also the only shelter for those fishermen working the Fairweather grounds off the coast. Tlingit people knew of the bad karma of the place and there were tales of a sea monster at the bottom of the bay that shook the place, causing earthquakes and giant waves.

Nearly two hundred years later, Don J. Miller of the US Geological Survey, who had heard of the wave legends, postulated that the waves were the products of earthquakes. So to explore his theory he measured tree rings in the forest surrounding Lituya. When he mapped his results, he found contour lines of trees of the same age, indicating that big waves periodically stripped the forest bare on the shores of the bay.

Not many scientists paid attention to his theories until the big wave of 1958. On July 9 of that year, a huge tsunami blew out of Lituya Bay in coastal Alaska. A 7.8-level earthquake along the Fairweather fault shook down an estimated 30 million tons of rock into the north arm of Lituya Bay. The rocks displaced water that drove the glacier, which was terminating in that end of the bay, to rise up hundreds of feet and when it came down it shot a wave down into the bay. Mature forests were stripped of their trees at one location to a height of 1,720 feet. It was the highest-known wave ever witnessed.

You read that correctly. There were witnesses. Three commercial fishing boats were anchored in the bay. Some fishermen were lost when their fishing boat went down. Two other people were washed over the trees on the sand spit, got off their sinking boat, and rowed an eight-foot pram around out in the open ocean until rescuers found them. The fishing vessel *Yakobi* survived the wave, and her captain and his son lived to tell the story. You can read their account in a government publication, *Giant Waves in Lituya Bay, Alaska*, by Don J. Miller.

Miller's prediction had come true. Ten years after the earthquake, I was at Lituya in my duties as a national park ranger. I took aerial photos of the wave damage, and I hiked the areas surrounding the bay, checking on mining claims and bear poaching. Due to the tides, the onshore waves, and a diagonal channel with many rocks on each side, Lituya Bay has the most dangerous bay entrance I have experienced, and it has claimed the lives of many sailors.

A Night in a Log Jam and a Week of Beach Time
We had gone on the MV *Nunatak* to Lituya Bay to check on a placer mining camp up the coast near Cape

Fairweather. Chief Ranger Chuck Janda and I were taken ashore in a skiff and dropped off for a hike up the coast and back. Bruce Paige, the park naturalist, was with us, intending to do some collecting of small rodents for the park's reference collection. As the skiff headed back to the *Nunatak*, a huge blow started to come in from the sea. It carried gusts measured on the boat's anemometer as high as 75 miles per hour. The captain pulled up anchor and moved the boat behind Cenotaph Island for shelter.

Chuck and I hiked for two or three hours and, seeing the storm was blowing hard, knew we were not getting picked up that evening, so we spent the night in one of the miners' wall tents. Bruce, however, was not so lucky. A sow brown bear with cubs wandered by his location and showed some aggressive moves to protect her cubs. To protect himself, Bruce climbed into a large logjam left from the 1958 wave and spent a cold, wet night hiding from the bear. When Chuck and I found him in the morning he was shivering and doing calisthenics on the beach, waiting for his pickup. We all got a hot meal on the boat and Bruce had a story to tell.

During bear hunting season we received a tip that illegal game guides based in Yakutat were poaching Alaska brown bears on the beaches between Sea-Otter Creek on the northern end of the park and Cape Fairweather. Bruce Paige and I were assigned to spend a week hiking the north coastal beaches to discourage the poachers. The informant told us the guides were flying big-wheeled planes that could land on the beach. When they spotted bears foraging on the beach, they would land the poachers near enough for a shot. The dead bear would be skinned and the head and hide flown back to Yakutat and forwarded to a taxidermist for trophy preparation. Not only were park regulations being violated, but the concept of "fair chase" embodied in the hunting tradition was being ignored by using the aircraft as an auxiliary hunting tool.

Layton Bennet from Haines flew us out in his Piper Super Cub with big beach tires on it. The fabric in the rear section had a hole in it, and Bruce got some unexpected sightseeing along the way. Looking down through the hole he could see the big surf crashing into the cape. It wasn't comforting. On the way out, Layton handed back a bag of peanuts and two orange sodas, shouting to us that this was a first-class flight. We landed on the beach and the sand was a little soft, so Layton taxied slowly while we pitched our gear out and jumped from the rolling Piper as he gunned the engine and took off.

Bruce and I were instructed to wear our ranger uniforms and be visible. We had been supplied with an old army radio, but it didn't work, so we were on our own for the week. We camped in a spot where we would be visible to passing aircraft. I packed a high-powered rifle and Bruce had a strong pair of binoculars. When aircraft would fly over, he'd read the registration numbers out loud and I'd write them down. The coast was a relatively busy route for small aircraft. One could avoid crossing the Saint Elias Range by flying down the beaches and either cutting into Cross Sound, or going on to Sitka. Many aircraft would waggle their wings when they spotted us as a hello, but a few would peel off when they saw us and head back north. We suspected those were the culprits.

During that week, we hiked and climbed along the coast and back a considerable distance. Our footprints in the sand could be seen above the high-tide line for miles in both directions. There were also footprints of bears out there and some were enormous. How big? I fit both of my boots into one big footprint and spent the rest of that afternoon looking over my shoulder. Bruce, who is the best birder I know, was having a hard time figuring out what he was seeing as thousands of shorebirds passed us flying low and at very high speed on their northward migration. That was also the time I learned about the magnitude of the winter storms and freak waves along the coast. On the steep portion of Cape Fairweather we found driftwood logs stuck in the trees more than 100 feet in elevation above the beach.

Behind Cape Fairweather we found a huge sinkhole hundreds of feet in diameter and perhaps 100 feet deep. Trees were tumbled into piles where they had been uprooted and fallen into the hole. We surmised that the forest had grown on the dirt and rock surface of a glacier for many years. As the runoff from the retreating ice melted the underlying ice, the forest was suspended over an empty space. At a certain point the whole structure must have collapsed. Evidence of sinkholes like this can be found in Wisconsin and other places that were once covered by ice, but I don't think I have seen anything quite as big as this one. We backed away from the edge as carefully as we could.

At the end of the week, Layton Bennet came to get us in a tricycle-geared plane that couldn't carry all of our gear. So we left our equipment cached above the tide line and flew home. Layton later made a second trip for the gear. We learned from various sources that there was a rumor that the Park Service had brought a "flying squad" of rangers up from Yosemite to cover the beaches and stop poachers. We had been spotted in so many places that it seemed as if there were more rangers than just Bruce and me!

CHAPTER 16

From Glaciers to Volcanoes — Katmai

It was late in the spring of 1969. I got a call from the regional office asking me to go to Katmai National Monument to fill in for the park ranger who had been evacuated because of a bleeding ulcer. That was "park ranger" — singular. I would be the only permanent ranger. Worse, my family had to stay at Glacier Bay because there was only a small one-room cabin available at the park.

Katmai is on the Alaska Peninsula across the Shelikof Strait from Kodiak Island. It is an enormous park, 4,000-plus square miles in size and goes nearly all the way north across the Alaska Peninsula to Bristol Bay. The park contains many active volcanic areas, including Mount Katmai, which collapsed during the explosive 1912 eruption at Novarupta Volcano, forming the Valley of 10,000 Smokes as well as a crater lake. The park is home to hundreds of Alaska brown bears, wolves, moose, wolverines, and many other creatures. Millions of sockeye salmon return to its lake systems every year, and many migratory birds nest there.

I flew to Anchorage, got my orders from the superintendent, and flew to King Salmon Air Field where the National Park Service had a bunkroom and

small shop. I launched one of the
north end of Naknek Lake, tossed m
of food supplies in, and ran the ten m
Camp, the only ranger station in the p
built four simple cabins for employees
the Brooks River and Naknek Lake, a... one of them
was mine. There was a small visitor lodge that could
hold a dozen or so people and a small four-wheel drive
bus to take people on an all-day trip to the Valley of
10,000 Smokes.

The park had acquired a 32-foot landing craft to haul
fuel, supplies, and a couple of pieces of road
maintenance equipment from King Salmon to the park.
Other supplies and mail came on a daily Grumman
Mallard seaplane that carried eleven passengers and on
a Pilatus Porter turbo-prop float plane that could take
off and land in a hundred yards or so.

In the first couple of days, my seasonal ranger crew
showed up on the float plane. Sever Woll had been a
ranger the year before. Arnold Handshke was a
schoolteacher from Adak Naval Base who hadn't spent
time in the wilderness. The other two, Bonnie Koploy
and Diane Drigot, were college students from the
Midwest and Los Angeles, respectively. Neither of the
women rangers had been in Alaska before.

The Brooks Camp facility had been built on one of the
richest archaeological sites in Alaska. It was also astride
an active brown bear freeway, with daily visits from
some of the largest bears in the world. During an
orientation walk, Diane, one of the new rangers, asked

Hypothetical question. If an aggressive brown bear came down the trail now, what would you do?"

I answered immediately, "Trip you and run."

She scoffed at me. "No, really," I said. "Do you know how to operate the radio? Do you have a first-aid card? How about operating the boat?"

The answer to all three questions was, of course, no. I said, "I'm serious. Bears don't often kill people. They mostly maul them. So if the bear gets me, I'm screwed. But if the bear gets you and walks away, I can clean and even stitch your wounds, radio for an evacuation, and run you out in a skiff to meet a seaplane." That was enough for the seasonal rangers. First-aid classes started that evening on the steps at my cabin and people were anxious to learn the radio protocols and to become familiar with boat operations. And keep away from the bears.

Arnold Handshke's luggage was missing from his US Navy flight from Adak. He had no uniform so I lent him some of my shirts, pants, and my summer flat hat. I am stretching it to say that I'm an extra large. Arnie was a medium, and spent the summer in my spare uniforms looking like he had lost about a hundred pounds. Not only that, his head was a lot smaller than mine and if I recall, we had to put a jogging head-band inside the hat so it wouldn't blow off in a stiff breeze. As these things go, his luggage showed up two days prior to the end of the summer season, with tags indicating it had been sent all the way to Cam Ranh Bay in Vietnam before finally arriving in Alaska. He put on his brand-new uniform—which fit him perfectly—loaded up the VCR camera he had stored in his luggage, and walked around taking videos for two solid days.

The radio was squawking again, and when I answered it, the excited voice on the other end told me that that people were reporting smelling a strong odor of sulfur in Kodiak and I needed to fly over the park and check on possible eruptions. Residents of Kodiak have good reason to be nervous about eruptions. To put this in some perspective, during the 1912 eruption, six feet of ash fell on Kodiak, blackening the sky and covering the city. The city's residents sheltered below decks on the US Revenue Cutter *Bear* while men took turns shoveling to keep the decks clear. Below, they were reportedly singing "Nearer My God to Thee."

US Fish and Wildlife pilot Bill Pinette, one of the best small plane pilots around, picked me up and we headed across the mountains to do our volcano checks. About 30 minutes into the flight we banked over Trident Volcano and looked down into its crater. Where there had been a huge lava plug the previous week, there was now a steaming hole surrounded by the yellow stain of sulfur. The two cubic acres or so of lava that had been capping Trident the week before had blown into the air and we got the heck out of there before it spit out some more. Fortunately, there were no reports of volcanic bombs hitting anyone in the fishing fleet or elsewhere during that explosive eruptive phase, but we kept an eye out for flying lava or ash for the following week.

On some days, I would run the landing craft in to King Salmon to pick up supplies and barrels of fuel. Sever Woll was an experienced seasonal ranger and was left in charge in my absence. The boat was slow but reliable, and when it wasn't available, we would tie an old plywood cannery skiff to the side of a homemade barge and push it several miles into town and back using an aging 35-horsepower outboard engine. It was boring duty, but the whole lodge and park cabin complex was powered by a single five KW Witte one-cylinder diesel generator, and we needed the fuel for it and the bus, park boats, and equipment. Our entire camp was built on volcanic pumice, and when that old single-cylinder generator would operate, the ground would shake. I would feel like I was sleeping on one of those "Magic Fingers" coin-operated motel beds.

There were other dangers, too, and not nature based. The University of Alaska had a research operation going at Novarupta Volcano. The scientists were measuring the depth of the magma reservoir beneath the volcano's surface plug. An old Bell Ranger helicopter ferried scientists from our camp's beach out to the volcano camp. One day I was bringing an open skiff into the beach when I saw the helicopter revving up for takeoff. I paused 200 feet from the beach and watched as the aircraft rose up, tipped forward—and caught a rotor on the water. The rear of the chopper disintegrated as the big rotor descended into the tail section and a storm of metal and rotor fragments came flying at me. Nothing hit me, but a big piece of rotor flew much too close over my head and the image of the

Grim Reaper flashed through my mind as I ducked for cover.

The helicopter had tipped sideways in shallow water as I motored in to help. Fuel was spilling into the lake, and I cut the engine and grabbed a paddle and got to the helicopter. Just then I spotted the lodge manager running down the beach to help. He was carrying a lit cigarette in one hand and was headed for the leaking fuel. I shouted at him to butt out the cigarette and come and help, which he did when he saw the leaking fuel. We waded to the busted chopper and got the hatch opened and the pilot and two geologists climbed out. Aside from a couple of scratches, everyone was okay. The following day, a big Sikorsky Sky-Crane came out and plucked the broken helicopter off the beach and carted it off to wherever dead helicopters go.

At the end of the season, I interviewed the geologists and asked them about their findings around Novarupta. Dr. Donald Stone told me we shouldn't build anything in the valley downslope. The magma was there waiting for the earth's hidden dispatch mechanism to set it off for another big blow. The big thing I learned from the scientists and from observation is that the earth's plumbing is complex. Most good predictions of eruptive behavior are made after the shaking and minor venting begins. But exactly where and when the blowout will come is never absolutely certain. The Katmai volcanoes are some of the easternmost of the complex of Aleutian chain volcanoes, and they are some of the most explosive.

Working at Glacier Bay and Katmai gave me a different perspective about life and the planet we inhabit. For all the massive changes we undertake as a species, we are actually temporary leaseholders. The ice has scoured the northern hemisphere more than once and volcanic eruptions have covered great sections of North America in the past. Long ago the sea moved into the center of our continent and I am willing to bet it will do so again. It's a hollow wager, because I won't be here to either pay up or collect.

VIPs

One day, the superintendent called on the radio from Anchorage to tell me that two important guests were headed my way a week apart. The first was Robert Cahn, a reporter from the *Christian Science Monitor*. Bob Cahn had just won a Pulitzer Prize for a series of feature articles entitled "Will Success Spoil the National Parks?" In the series he outlined the archaic facilities and lack of staffing in national parks. He was up in Alaska to have a look at one of America's most remote parks. The director had called Anchorage and requested VIP treatment.

On that same day, a plane loaded with well-dressed Italian tourists had flown in during the morning. My practice was to meet the planes and give a short talk on bear safety as visitors disembarked. Only one person of the group spoke English, though, and before I could get anyone's attention, they spotted a bear and began yelling in Italian and running down the beach, pulling their cameras out of their bags. I anticipated the worst, but evidently so did the bear. Faced with a dozen running and yelling Italian tourists, the huge brown bear prudently wheeled around and went crashing off to the hills at a high rate of speed. I got the Italians safely into the lodge and prepared for my first VIP.

Bob Cahn was dropped off on the beach by one of Wein Airlines's float planes. When he stepped ashore, I saw a small balding man with glasses and a serious look on his face. From the start, I knew he wasn't comfortable in the wilds of Katmai. What I didn't know was that Bob Cahn was the keenest observer of what was going on that I would ever meet. I learned that he had been an officer in a tank division during World War II, and he had served as a White House correspondent during the Kennedy years. Bob told me that he had been the first person to get an exclusive interview with Marilyn Monroe and Joe DiMaggio after their wedding. But he was a little nervous about going flying with me that afternoon.

Bill Pinette picked us up in a Cessna float plane and we flew off through the mountains to the coast where we counted bears. In a ten-mile stretch of the south coast of the park we counted fifty-three Alaskan brown bears. As we flew over at a couple hundred feet, a huge male bear stood on his hind legs and took a swat at us. *That* was a bear I didn't want to meet. We also spotted the famous horse that had been dropped off when a vessel carrying a few horses anchored in one of the bays and put the horses ashore to forage while they repaired the engine. One horse could not be found when they reloaded, and here he was twelve years later, all shaggy and proud having survived severe winters and all those brown bears.

We turned and headed for home, but while we had been flying, the weather had dropped a cloud curtain down in the passes through the mountains and we had to turn south, drop down into Kukak Bay, and beach the float plane until the weather cleared. In a tidal area, a float plane requires a lot of attention to make sure the floats don't end up high and dry on the beach. So I started a campfire while Bill tended to the plane. Bob got pretty nervous and worried about all the bears we had seen. First, he asked where we'd sleep and I told him I was just planning to sit by the fire. He wasn't happy about it so we put him in the airplane. "What will we eat?" he called from the plane. I tossed him one of the two candy bars I always carried when in the bush and he settled down.

When the low clouds had risen a little, we doused the fire, got in the plane, and headed back toward Brooks Camp. There was a narrow open triangle of clear space in one of the passes and Bill turned the Cessna on its side and shot through the hole into the clear. He later told me that Bob's nervousness was driving him crazy and he just wanted to get us out of his plane. It felt like he was going to do it the hard way! That evening Bob and I sat for most of the night and talked about Katmai, Glacier Bay, and the needs of the National Park System. It was the beginning of a long friendship. When he returned to Washington, DC, he wrote an article asking why a 4,000-square mile park with more than a dozen active volcanoes and one of the world's greatest wildlife populations had only one permanent ranger.

My next VIP was Undersecretary of Interior Russell E. Train. Mr. Train was in Alaska holding hearings on the proposed haul-road for construction of the Alaska Pipeline. He was also chairing hearings regarding the impending nuclear tests deep beneath Amchitka Island. Mr. Train had his family along and we had some wonderful trips to watch beavers constructing a lodge and other sights. Later alongside the fireplace in the lodge, Mr. Train spent a lot of time asking me questions about Alaska and some of the issues he was there to study. I believe he wanted to hear the views of someone on the ground who was not connected to the projects. The visit of those two VIPs was to have huge consequences in my future.

The End of Summer
There were to be a couple more adventures before I headed home for the winter. I hauled a brand-new 20-KW Kohler generator out to the park to replace the old Witte. The generator had made the long trip north on a barge and we were lucky to get it before winter. We wrestled the machine up to the generator shed and I took the instruction sheets back to my cabin to read over dinner. Our mechanic, the only other permanent employee at Katmai, was incompetent. If I seem judgmental about him the following episode will prove my judgment. I told him to leave the machine alone until I got a look at the installation instructions.

As I sat in my cabin, eating some canned delight for dinner, I heard the diesel engine start up. Before I could run up to the shed to stop it, the light bulbs all flashed brightly and burned out. When I reached the shed, the mechanic had turned off the machine but it was too late. He had shot 220 volts throughout the 110-volt system and not only melted some plastic radios and tape players but messed up the electronics in the new generator so it could not be used. I was furious and the mechanic didn't last much longer in the Park Service. Technicians had to be flown in to repair the generator.

The other disaster had to do with boats. The park had two boats used by the rangers. One was an old plywood cabin cruiser with two brand-new 35-horse outboards hanging off the stern. The other was a trihedral fiberglass 16-footer with a V6 inboard/outboard engine. Ranger Handshke and I took the boats to King Salmon for mail and supplies and to drop off the old plywood skiff at the shop. It didn't survive the trip. About halfway to town, the wind came up, and the boats began to take a beating. Arnold was in the plywood boat, which began to open a seam in the bottom and take on water.

I switched boats with him, cut the top out of an empty five-gallon fuel can, and bailed until the water level was down. I then ran the boat for a while until it was too full and repeated the whole procedure. Arnold followed at a distance as I ran the runabout toward shore, hoping to beach the skiff. As soon as the lake water depth got shallow enough, I shut the motors down, jumped into the lake and waded toward shore, towing the boat with a rope. Arnold saw me from a distance and thought I had fallen over. He goosed the throttle and came roaring in to save me. Going about 30 miles per hour his boat hit a rock that punctured the hull and broke the outdrive, shutting down the motor. To say it was a bad moment would be an understatement.

We towed both boats ashore and I pulled the outboards from the wooden skiff and stashed them in the bushes for future pickup. We stuffed rags in the hole and rigged the auxiliary ten-horse outboard on the damaged fiberglass boat, and in the middle of the night, Arnold and I motored in to King Salmon at a very slow pace, arriving exhausted. I spent the rest of the night writing accident reports, bummed a ride back to Brooks Camp, and began to shut down the operation for the end of the season. The cold was coming down from the ridges and winter was coming on in a hurry. Seasonals were given their evaluations, winterizing was done, and we left for our homes.

I lost track of three of the seasonal rangers, but Diane Drigot became a long-time friend. She did a master's degree with research on visitor attitudes in wilderness areas, went on to earn a doctorate at the University of Michigan, and had a career as the environmental manager at the Kaneohe Marine Base on Oahu. Diane was given several national awards for her work with the Marines. In 2013 she passed away from leukemia at age 65 in her adopted home of Hawai'i.

Back at Glacier Bay

My family welcomed me back to Bartlett Cove in late September. I spent the fall and winter helping replace outdrives on the patrol boat and doing the winter tasks that are not glamorous but certainly necessary. We bundled up and visited remote weather stations that were able to measure accumulated snowfall and rain volumes. We continued our surveys of snow depths on the glaciers and sent the data to researchers at the Ohio State Institute for Polar Studies for use in making long-term weather projections. I looked forward to the coming summer season, but a letter from Bob Cahn changed that plan.

CHAPTER 17

Summer Visitors at Katmai

Robert Cahn and Russell Train, my two summer visitors at Katmai, had been appointed by President Richard Nixon to join Dr. Gordon J.F. MacDonald as the first members of the President's Council on Environmental Quality. The council, put together as part of the National Environmental Policy Act (NEPA), was charged with developing the rules for NEPA and working as principal advisors to the President on such matters. There was no budget for the council in its first year, so the council members went fishing in the pool of federal employees and borrowed some of us for the first year. I was asked to be a staff biologist.

Some perspective is necessary here. I was a full-time law enforcement officer with a wife and three children when I earned my bachelor's degree in biology at San Jose State College. My grades were above average but not by a lot. I once got a case of beer and celebrated with fellow students when I received a C-minus in cellular physiology. I didn't consider myself a mediocre student, but I'm sure some people did. Bob Cahn told me he wanted someone with field experience who understood the contentious issues surrounding national parks and wildlife refuges, and that I did. I kissed Susie good-bye, leaving her to pack the household and follow later, boarded a float plane, and wove my way via the airlines from Juneau to Washington, DC.

A day later, American Airlines dropped me off at Dulles Airport at 12:30 a.m. and I grabbed my backpack off the baggage carousel and caught an airporter bus to downtown. I had no hotel reservations and no idea what I was heading into. On the bus, a kind fellow federal employee saw my backpack with an Alaska luggage tag and struck up a conversation with me. He was shocked to discover that I had come into town without a reservation and offered to help me find a room at the place he was staying. So at 2 a.m. we were dropped off at the Albert Pick-Lee hotel in downtown DC. The entrance was locked and guarded, we discovered. Our bus had rumbled through the devastated downtown area where recent riots had burned storefronts, and a lot of stores were still boarded up. Quite a change from Bartlett Cove!

The hotel was full, but when the night manager heard my story, he found a sofa for me in a small room off the lobby for the night. The following day I was moved to a room that would be my home for the following month. The next morning was spent at Woodward & Lothrop's department store, where I spent $120 on a cheap blue suit, a tie, and two dress shirts. I had brought my old Army-issue black dress shoes and found a shop to get them resoled, and before the day was over I looked in the mirror and observed the $140 transformation of a national park ranger into a bureaucrat in a cheap suit.

The council was temporarily housed on the first floor of a building a few blocks from the White House. We were working downstairs from the Pornography Commission. Later we would move to a renovated townhouse across the street from Lafayette Park, half a block from the White House. I reported for duty and found that I was the fifth person hired, and the only biologist. An office was provided, and I was introduced to Janet Peck, my secretary. As a GS-7 park ranger, I was amused to discover my salary level was lower than hers. This was my first lesson on who actually knows how to run the government. Jan was one of a corps of professional support staff without whom the massive wheels of government would grind to a halt. I met with the three council members and was given the title of Staff Member for Environmental Pollution. Al Alm, the chief of staff, had made the title up on the spot, and he walked me to my office and gave me the first environmental impact statements (EIS) filed under NEPA and told me to review them.

If my recollection is accurate, the first EIS filed was regarding the effects of a multi-story development on the National Park Service property on Theodore Roosevelt Island in the Potomac River (not to be mistaken with Roosevelt Island in the East River in New York City). It was a terrible attempt to get past the requirements of NEPA before anyone noticed. It also triggered a meeting with the director of the National Park Service and Bob Cahn to figure out where we were headed with this whole environmental quality deal. Director Hartzog had no idea who I was, even though he had assigned me. I got a close-up view of how things worked at the top.

The next week I had a meeting with Chief Edward P. Cliff of the US Forest Service after I sent their first EIS back as unacceptable. Louisiana Pacific Corp. was proposing a pulp mill at Echo Cove north of Juneau, Alaska. I had opened my mouth the week before and was quoted in the newspapers saying that L.P. Corp. had done more work on the environmental impacts of the plant than the Forest Service had. By the end of my first week, I had become a source of amusement around the council office with my unique ability to function with my foot in my mouth.

About ten days into my assignment, Al Alm told me to accompany him to a meeting. The first project in our charge of giving advice to the President was to be a study of the effects of dumping in the ocean. It turned out that we were dumping everything from urban garbage and sewage plus an amazing array of other stuff into our oceans. Al introduced me to a group of senior government officials seated around a long conference table and told them that I would be the staff person assigned to chair the meetings and write the report. Then he left the room.

Surprise is too mild a word to describe my feelings. *Flabbergasted* is more like it. The man seated on my left was Dr. Leslie Glasgow, the Assistant Secretary of Interior, who supervised the National Parks director. The others at the table held equally august positions and yet I was in charge. The people around the table quickly figured me for a fraud with good reason. I faked it by asking to be brought up to speed on where each agency was on the study, took a few illegible notes, scheduled the next week's meeting, and left in somewhat of a daze.

I believed I was out of my depth so I talked to Al about the project and he told me to get what work product I could from the committee and write the report. He assigned Charles F. Lettow, a young lawyer (now a federal judge) who had clerked for Chief Justice Warren Burger at the US Supreme Court to help with the legal aspects, including any draft legislation. Chuck Lettow and I attended the next meeting and found that most participants had brought excuses about why their agency didn't have time or resources to participate in the project and had sent low-level surrogates in their places. The message was, "*You* do it!"

What happened next was a lot of fun. My recollection is that Chuck suggested we simply draft a bill that would get their attention. We sat down and put together a bill that banned everything. No more dredge spoil disposal by the Army Corps of Engineers. No dumping of radioactive pressure vessels by the Atomic Energy Commission. New York would have to quit dumping sewage into the New York Bight, where a toxic biological desert had been created. We passed out the draft at the following meeting—and the poop hit the proverbial fan. Participants picked up the drafts and left. The following day, I heard that Admiral Hyman G. Rickover was quoted in the newspaper saying, "If this bill becomes law I won't be able to p— off the fantail of an aircraft carrier!" Suddenly, the principal committee members showed up and began to work as part of a team to address not only the current issues but future ones as well.

Briefings were scheduled with council members by agencies that wanted to keep dumping materials in the sea. The City of Boston hired the Mudge, Rose law firm to come down to convince us that it would be fine to dump all of Boston's garbage at depths of thousands of feet in the Atlantic. It didn't require more than high school physics to see through the childish charts showing their scheme and I said so. Unbeknownst to me, I had again become the source of amusement because I didn't realize we were being touted by the President's old law firm! But there was never any blowback from the White House on any of this, and I believe that for all of President Nixon's faults, his record on the environment was stellar.

The Monster in the White House Basement

Al Alm sent me a college student intern named David Yesnir to help with the report. Al thought he would be a "gopher," but instead I put him to work drafting portions of the report we had been cobbling together. I remember David as a wisecracking student with a cheap suit and a good mind. After he got over the shock of knowing he could be making national policy, he settled down and did some remarkable work.

White House report deadlines were draconian. We pulled some all-nighters and worked weekends. One

Sunday I was frantically trying to copy 40 or so pages of the draft for distribution on Monday morning. Our copy machine couldn't handle the work, so I asked the people on duty at the White House where I could get access to a big copier.

And thus I found myself alone in the basement of the White House facing an enormous, state-of-the-art Xerox machine. Today, I can print ten copies of a 40-page document at home on a machine that cost $125 plus ink. In 1970, however, the work was done on a machine the size of a pickup truck turned on its side. Copies were shot out onto a collating stack by noisy mechanical arms of some kind. I punched in the numbers, hit copy, and immediately, papers started flying into the stacker. Papers! Lots and lots of papers! I discovered that I had inadvertently hit an extra digit so instead of 400 pieces of paper it was spitting out 4,000.

I panicked and couldn't stop the damned thing, no matter which button I pushed, so I ran around and pulled the plug, finally shutting the whole thing down. I removed what copies had been made and reported to the head clerical person in the working offices upstairs what had happened. She gave me a very long look and told me it took about two hours to restart the monster machine. Doing so apparently required someone to climb on a platform, take a paddle, and stir a big reservoir of toner in order to get it going again. I offered to paddle but she sent me away. At the morning staff meeting I found out amongst much hilarity that I had been banned from the White House basement. It was a dubious distinction, because no one else on the staff had ever even been in the basement, let alone seen the monster machine. I got to participate in two briefings of President Nixon after that, but all were on the first floor.

I was proud of our 40 pages and the new legislation Chuck Lettow and a fellow named Bill Lake had put together. The report looked incredibly spare to me. No extra gobbledygook. Then we turned it over to an editor from the Government Printing Office. With a hard deadline coming up, the editor worked quickly and returned the thing to us. It was now sixteen pages. What happened to the other 24 pages? The editor told me to read it and if I found anything missing I should tell her within two hours and we'd work on it. Try as I did, I could find nothing missing except all my extra verbiage, so I signed off.

The next week we briefed President Nixon and the ocean dumping bill was sent to the Congress as Presidential request legislation. But wait! The bill was already there, having been introduced by Senator Edmund Muskie of Maine. Someone had leaked it and I was immediately a suspect. I received an interrogation visit from White House political staff. I told them it wasn't me but they persisted in questioning me. I recall getting indignant, standing up and telling them to look elsewhere for a rat and that I had a lot of work to do and they needed to butt out. Again, no repercussions. I never did find out who the leak was.

The rest of my year on loan was filled with work. On one occasion or another I attended meetings and did briefings with all of the principals eventually implicated in the Watergate scandal. I can say without reservation that they were actively developing an environmental quality reputation for President Nixon, and with the exception of a couple of political flunkies, I was treated with respect and collegiality during my assignment.

National Park Service Director George Hartzog asked me to come and talk to him. I walked over to the Interior Department and received another in the series of surprises my career had turned into. "Are you an American Indian?" the director asked. I told him I was part Native Hawai'ian. He was astounded and told me he had no idea there were any Hawai'ian rangers and that he was being hammered by Hawai'ian activists because Hawai'ians occupied only menial or lower-level jobs in the parks. And there I had been all this time! We had a nice talk, and he sent me back to my office.

On my bus ride to work the following morning I read in the *Washington Post* that Secretary of Interior Walter Hickel had been fired because of his letter criticizing President Nixon over the Vietnam War. Director Hartzog called again and I walked over again to Interior to find the place all abuzz. Assistant Secretary Leslie Glasgow had also been fired and was packing to return to his college professorship at Louisiana State University.

George Hartzog invited me into his office and said, "I want you to go to Maui." I figured he had some project he wanted me to accomplish and I asked, "What do you want me to do?" The director, a large man, put his hand on my shoulder and said, "I want you to be superintendent of Haleakala National Park."

If I were a smaller man you could have knocked me over with a feather. "I don't know anything about the business of being a superintendent," I said.

"That's why you have an administrative officer. You can learn on the job," he said.

It turned out that George knew his days were numbered and was pulling all of his people who might also be vulnerable back into the career service. Two years after I had been transferred, George Hartzog, the best director the service ever had, was fired and replaced by Ron Walker, a former insurance executive and the man who planned the President's travel arrangements. Mr. Walker served for two years and was replaced shortly after President Nixon's resignation.

The people in the Interior Secretary's office did me a big favor and used an obscure section of the personnel rules to advance me to a pay grade just below the superintendent's level and promised me a raise after I succeeded on the job for a year. I was doing important things in DC, but the dream of managing a great national park in the place my ancestors had lived was too tempting. I left the council staff on the last day of 1970, dusted off my uniform, packed up the family, and moved 5,000 miles from one end of the country to the other.

CHAPTER 18

The House of the Sun — 1971

Haleakala National Park commands the summit of the East Maui volcanic mass. Together with Hawai'i Volcanoes National Park, it was one of the original parks established in 1916 when the Park Service in its present form was established. The Seven Pools area at Kipahulu was added to the park in recent years and the park now ranges from the seashore up to more than 10,000 feet of elevation. Sometimes there can be bikini weather at the shore and an ice storm at the top.

The view from the top of the mountain is gorgeous. People get up at three a.m. and drive the winding road to the summit just to experience the sunrise. On clear days visitors can see the nearby islands of Hawai'i, Kahoolawe, and Lanai. The character of the place that drew such raves from Mark Twain when he rode a horse to the summit was centered in the view of the crater. Geologists tell us that it's not really a crater, but is a meeting of two headward eroding valleys. But no one really cares what they say. To locals and visitors it's "the Crater."

One Hawai'ian myth that the rangers tell says that the demigod Maui was perturbed because the sun traveled too fast for his mother's tapa cloth to dry, so he lassoed the sun from inside the crater and caused it to slow to its present cycle. Regardless of the myth's provenance, the crater is sacred to Hawai'ians. There were many local stories of Hawai'ians traveling on foot to a volcanic vent and leaving the umbilical cord of their newborn child in the vent hole. There is also plenty of archaeological evidence that the crater was the repository for the bones of early Hawai'ians.

Most of the park is rugged back country, accessible on foot or horseback. A walk or ride through the crater is like a trip to the moon. Craters and volcanic cones are scattered about, along with lava tubes and brightly colored remnants of old volcanic spatter. Astronauts for the Apollo space program trained there to get a feeling for what the moon's surface would be like. Foot and horse travelers could camp in three places where rustic bunkrooms had been built many years before. Reservations for bunk spaces filled up months before scheduled trips.

The Hawai'i National Parks were first proposed in 1903 by Lorrin Thurston, one of the architects of the overthrow of the Hawai'ian monarchy. The proposal languished until Prince Jonah Kuhio Kalaniana'ole, Hawai'i's Congressional delegate, worked it through various Congressional committees. In 1915 Thurston and volcanologist Thomas Jagger spent time showing the park proposals to a delegation of 124 visiting Congressmen. Prince Kuhio's bill passed Congress and was signed into law on August 1, 1916.

Thurston and Kalaniana'ole have to be two of the oddest political allies in American history. Thurston led a movement of missionary descendants and white merchants that overthrew the duly elected constitutional monarchy and helped reconstruct it into a government run by his peers. They passed laws disenfranchising most of the Native Hawai'ians. He became a wealthy and influential man.

Prince Kuhio Kalaniana'ole plotted for the overthrow of the government formed by the "Bayonet Constitution," as Thurston's movement was referred to, and was convicted of treason and sentenced to death. He and the other plotters were given clemency and a year in prison. On his release, the prince went to England and joined the British army, fighting in the Boer War in South Africa. When he returned to Hawai'i, he joined the Home Rule Party, ran for election, and served ten terms as Hawai'i's nonvoting delegate in the US Congress. Without voting power, Prince Kuhio developed a poker table strategy. He rented space for a men's club near the Capitol and, with his wife providing refreshments, hosted Congressmen for poker games. It is my belief that Prince Kuhio's political success was largely accomplished at the poker table.

My first meeting with staff was somewhat prophetic. I was introduced to the chief ranger, who was smoking a cigarette in one of those FDR cigarette holders. He shook my hand, turned to the other employees, and said, "Superintendents, they come and they go." Then he turned and walked back to his office. It wasn't a good start and it didn't get a lot better.

The remainder of the staff made up in positive energy what the chief ranger produced in negative. Jerome "Jerry" Pratt, the administrative officer, was the secretary of the Whooping Crane Society and a lifelong bird preservation guy. He was a retired Army lieutenant colonel and I believe he was the last commander of the Signal Corps carrier pigeon program. Yes, there was such a thing! From the Civil War until the end of World War II, pigeons had been used to carry secure messages. Jerry had loaded pigeons into aircraft being ferried long distances so a location could be sent in the event of an emergency landing. I heard that one of his pigeons traveled 5,000 miles with a message. At the end of WWII, as part of the occupation government, Jerry had been put in charge of one of the German zoos.

There was a stable of horses and old mules that carried freight and maintenance tools into the back-country cabins. The office support staff, wranglers, and maintenance crew were all local Maui people. Mixed in with the Native Hawai'ians were the descendants of Portuguese, Japanese, Russian, Filipino, Chinese, and Spanish "hyphen" Americans who were mixed with Hawai'ian and Euro-Americans to form the greatest mixing bowl of races in the world. Most of them were descended from workers imported for plantation labor over the centuries. Every ethnic group of the polyglot local population of Maui was represented on that staff. My secretary, Susan Nikaido, was a local woman who had never been off the island. The receptionist, Adele Fevella, was a woman who could speak the king's English one moment and the musical cadences of the Portuguese, Japanese, Hawai'ian pidgin spoken on Maui when local folks came in. She knew everything that was happening on Maui and kept me up to date on the goings and comings of local politics. One memory that has struck with me over the years is that of the work ethic of my crew. Whatever they were assigned was done and done well.

Over the years, the Hawai'i national park system had developed a reputation as a colonial government. Until I arrived, every superintendent, park ranger, and park maintenance supervisor at Haleakala had been white. I am *hapa haole* (part Hawai'ian, part white). My friend Jerry Shimoda, a Japanese-American raised in Hawai'i, served as superintendent at Puuhonua National Historic Park at Honaunau on the island of Hawai'i (commonly known as the Big Island). My boss was Bob Barrel, a tall, patrician-looking New Englander with a great heart. He looked at one of his roles as an opportunity to bring Hawai'ians and other ethnic people of the islands into the mainstream of park management.

I was raised on the mainland and thus was under suspicion as a "coconut," a Hawai'ian version of "Uncle Tom." My local cousins bailed me out, fortunately. I had so many relatives on Maui and Molokai that they outvoted the skeptics and I was accepted in most circles. Among those activists who wanted to keep up the conflict I was able to get by because I am not easily intimidated.

My family and I rented a house in the Makawao area and got to know the island. Each week I would drive to Hana on the west side of the island to meet with Park Ranger Tom Vaughn, who managed the newly acquired area at the Seven Pools at Oheo. Tom had gotten to know the community and had begun recruiting Hawai'ians into park jobs that would lead to ranger status. One of them was Francis Kuailani, who was probably the first full-blooded Hawai'ian to become a ranger and who later served as superintendent at Kaloko-Honokohau on the Big Island. Francis was also a fine musician and played on many albums of Hawai'ian music until he passed away.

The Seven Pools in the Kipahulu District had become known as the Seven Sacred Pools. No one knew any reason for the sacredness except the woman who spun tales for visitors at the Hotel Hana Ranch. She was a wonderful storyteller and if you looked at the place through her eyes, you could imagine a sacredness without any difficulty. The beauty of the pools drew people willing to drive the difficult winding road from the more populated parts of Maui. On my weekly drive to Kipahulu, I often met terrified drivers coming the other way who were cringing at the dropoffs along the cliff areas. Once the visitors got to the pools, however, the enchanted beauty of the place erased any misgivings they may have suffered getting there. A hike uphill through a bamboo forest brought you to a picturesque waterfall and plunge pool. Then you could follow a series of falls and pools down to the sea and watch local kids and tourists diving and swimming in the clear waters.

Charles and Anne Morrow Lindbergh lived near the pools, and I often saw Mrs. Lindbergh mucking around in the mud with local Hawai'ian volunteers who were restoring the stone-lined taro patches in the park. Charles spent many of his days fishing with local fishermen. He led a somewhat reclusive life but was kind enough to break his longstanding dislike of parties to attend a Nature Conservancy reception held for the nature activist Cordelia May. That evening Ms. May donated funds to acquire a large land holding adjacent to the park. When Charles passed away in 1974, his pallbearers were his Hawai'ian fishing friends. He was laid to rest in the Hawai'ian cemetery at the little Palapala Ho'omau church near Kipahulu.

The Nature Conservancy (TNC) recognized the enormous natural values inherent at Kipahulu. On up the stream in almost inaccessible valleys were birds found nowhere else in the world. Mosquitoes brought in from foreign places had infected native birds with avian malaria. The only remaining native Maui forest birds are now only found high on the mountains above the mosquitoes' range.

The way The Nature Conservancy raised money at the time was interesting. Huey Johnson was the western region director of TNC. Huey would line up donors and bring them to Maui. I'd meet them at the airport and accompany them to the top of Haleakala and we'd backpack into the crater. I would be carrying premium beefsteaks and Maui potatoes in my pack, while Huey's pack was loaded with fine wines. When we reached the ranger cabin at Paliku, Huey would lead the donors up onto Kalapawili Ridge for a spectacular view of the area. By the time he had returned with the exhausted people, I'd have chilled the wine in a net bag in the water tank and had steaks cooking on a big iron skillet on the wood stove.

We'd wine and dine everyone until they were absolutely sated and incredibly vulnerable, and then Huey would make the "ask." "Wasn't that spectacular?" he'd ask. Our guests would sip some more wine and nod. "Don't you think it should be saved?" More nodding. "Why don't you write us a check?" And with that, checkbooks would come out, and four- and sometimes five-figure checks would be written before the people were allowed to crawl into their bunks and fall asleep. I never minded being the prop for these forays and Huey even helped wash the dishes.

Life in the parks was different from the usual American living, and lots of adjustments were necessary just to do the ordinary things. The Kipahulu District was a long and difficult drive from the park headquarters and our rangers, Tom Vaughn and later Gordon Joyce, did a good job of working with the community of Hawai'ians. Hana and Kipahulu were some of the last places of traditional Hawai'ian living. People fished and grew gardens and many worked at low-wage jobs at the hotel and ranch. Gordon married a Nigerian woman named Chinyere and my wife Susie learned to cook some delicious African meals as well as the Hawai'ian dishes. Chinyere got along very well with the Hawai'ians and Gordon brought her to stay with us when their child was due so she could be near the hospital in Wailuku.

Ancestors Disturbed

A friend called me and let me know that two teenaged boys from Pukalani had brought human skulls out of the park and were displaying them in their bedrooms. For a Hawai'ian person to do such a thing was unthinkable. But these boys were not Hawai'ians and instead looked at their finds as souvenirs. I had to find out, so I called and made an appointment to meet them. The boys lived in a subdivision of more or less standard American bungalows of the 1960s. At the home of one of the boys, I met with them and their parents. They brought out the old skulls and we looked at a map on which they were able to plot an approximate location of their finds. The Pacific archeologist at Honaunau kept secret maps of known burial sites, and I was able to pinpoint the source of the skulls, ascertaining that they most likely were from ancient Hawai'ians.

I asked the boys how they would feel if someone dug up their great-grandparents and stole the skulls. They reluctantly agreed that it would not be nice, and I asked them how I should feel if the skulls they had removed were *my* ancestors. It was a good teaching moment, and the following Saturday the two boys accompanied me on a long trek down into Haleakala to return the skulls to their owners.

It was a gorgeous Maui day when I picked the boys up and drove to the park. We carried water and some sandwiches and hiked down the trail and across the crater. The cave in question was well off the trail and hidden by mamane bushes and brush. Using the archaeologist's unpublished maps, supplemented by the boys' recollection, we found the cave the skulls had come from. The black lava fields around us were hot but the lava tube we crawled into was cool and we worked our way a couple of hundred feet down into the volcanic cavern. At its heart we found the rest of the two skeletal remains. I gave some thought to the fact that these boys may have lacked a social conscience, but the crawl in was pretty tough and they certainly didn't lack a sense of curiosity and adventure.

Hawai'ians had once been known to carry the remains of the *alii* — the ruling class — up into the crater and hide them in the backs of the caves. The hiding was to prevent the royal bones from being carved by their enemies into fish hooks or other things. These two may have been alii. A big problem arose when I tried to figure out which head went on which body. Neither I nor the boys wanted some Hawai'ian curse to follow us around, so we did the best we could to match the heads with the rest. Satisfied we had done what we could, we crawled out of the cave, dusted off our clothes, and headed home.

A day hike into and out of the crater is not easy. But the day had cooled a little as the shadows covered the Halemau'u trail above Holua and after we had worked our way up to the road, I drove the two tired boys to their homes. Their parents were pleased that the boys were let off with warnings and I believed the boys were headed down the straight and narrow. I've always hoped we got the heads on the correct skeletons.

Nights on Haleakala

Some of the cleanest air in the world can be found two miles above sea level at the highest point on East Maui. Together with Mauna Loa and Mauna Kea on the Big Island, these sites are some of the best in the world for astronomical observation. There is plenty of evidence on these ridges that precontact Hawai'ians made observations from the high peaks and used the knowledge in navigating the great canoes between Hawai'i and Polynesia. One peak above the crater rim to the south of the summit is known to Hawai'ians as *Ke alaloa o' Kahiki* — the road to Tahiti. There is an old story that bonfires were lit up there on nights when voyagers were departing for a trip to the south, and it enabled ancient navigators to line up with navigational stars for their initial direction finding. Another explanation for the name may be that Polynesians all over the Pacific use cognates of the word *hawaiki* to indicate a source of their migration. Maori people have a belief that, upon death, their spirits travel north to '*Te Rerenga Wairua*, the north cape of the North Island of New Zealand, and return to Hawaiki. Tahiti, Hawaiki, and Hawai'i, among other similar words in Samoan and Tongan languages, seem to refer to the same place or concept of origin.

Because of the clean air up on the summit, today's astronomers have constructed observatories on the various peaks where serious research is conducted. During the Apollo missions, astronauts left reflective material on the moon. Scientists on Haleakala aimed laser beams at the reflectors and timed the returning laser beam. The experiments gave an accurate distance from the moon to the earth, and combined with data from other observatories, gave some new perspective on the shape of the earth. It's not as round as we thought.

Nights on Haleakala are often magical. There are no outside lights visible from within the crater. A pair of good binoculars is all that's needed to see many planets. I crawled out of my tent in the middle of one night at a campsite at Holua to look at the night sky, and some of the stars looked huge compared to those seen on other nights. They were like the stars in Van Gogh's paintings. When the French were acting stupid and setting off nuclear tests in French Polynesia, we stayed up late on the mountain and observed a Technicolor sky like no other. Those of us on the islands were probably subjected to increased radioactivity as well.

In December 1973, we gathered the children and blankets and traveled up the mountain to observe the comet Kohoutek. This comet, which hadn't been around the Earth's orbit for an estimated 150,000 years and wouldn't be back for another 75,000, was widely expected to be spectacular. We joined dozens of other Mauians and snuggled together under tarps and blankets in the cold at 9,000- or 10,000-feet elevation and waited. I scanned the heavens with binoculars for hours, but Kohoutek was a no-show, at least for us. The only good views were taken through the big telescopes and, I believe, by astronauts. A cult group called the Children of God claimed the comet was a precursor to the end of days, which would happen in forty days. I think I recall spending the fortieth day at the new McDonald's in Kahului. In the event they were right, we figured we'd go out enjoying a Big Mac.

Today, there is conflict over the use of these mountaintop sites. Native Hawai'ians consider them sacred and have picketed the construction of an enormously expensive telescope being built on the island of Hawai'i. Complaints about the carelessness of planners and operators and a collection of discarded junk around these important cultural sites are valid and show a lack of respect for the Hawai'ian culture. Only time will tell what the outcome of the disputes will be.

CHAPTER 19

Maui's Environment

When the English explored the Pacific in the latter part of the 18th century they worried about surviving shipwrecks and being marooned without food. Captain Vancouver, one of the great English navigators, decided to do something about it. He carried a supply of goats to islands all over the Pacific and left them there to forage, believing that shipwrecked sailors could hunt them for survival food. When he got to Hawai'i, the ruling chiefs reminded him that they had been promised cows during a previous visit. Vancouver was apparently out of cows so instead, he gave them goats. The Hawai'ian word for goat is *kau* (pronounced "cow"). I have always wondered...

The result of Vancouver's gift has been so successful that the goats have managed to alter the fragile isolated ecosystems on islands all over the Pacific Ocean. In Hawai'i they have mowed down the native plants, often leaving an area looking as if a giant lawn mower has passed by. When I arrived at Haleakala National Park, there were an estimated 3,000 goats in the 30,000 acres of the park. The result of their grazing was easy to see. Native plants were chewed off as fast as they could grow.

To try to control the goats and their destructive tendencies, park employees killed them on a regular basis. We carried rifles on patrols and shot them when we saw them. But they reproduced quickly and the population remained right around the big number. Goats weren't the only invasions into the ecosystem. A local man named Robert Kokubun was hired as a park technician whose principal job was getting the goat population down, and trapping feral cats and dogs that preyed on the young of rare seabirds that nested high on the mountain. We even tried using New Zealand experts with their sheep dogs that had been trained to round up feral animals in that island nation. Unfortunately, goats were well adapted to the terrain, and the slopes they frequented were too steep and the lava was tough on the dogs' feet. The handlers even sewed leather booties for their dogs, but the dogs still had limited success. Poisoning was considered, but the potential for damage to the park's rare species ruled that out.

We needed a serious remedy. Local hunters were experts at goat hunting, and jerked goat meat was a staple food in rural Maui. When word got out that the hunting option was being considered to keep the goat population to manageable numbers, the Sierra Club and others went ballistic. The precedent of using sport hunters in a national park was anathema to environmentalists. I didn't like it either, but the alternative was to see the native habitat disappear down the gullet of an animal that shouldn't be in the park anyway.

Nobody, including me, wanted to see any rule changes on hunting in the parks. We cobbled up a system where we deputized licensed hunters, gave them an orientation safety class, and sent them out on low-visitation days to kill goats. After three years of the program, we got the numbers down to about 300. It took more than twenty years and an incredibly difficult job of fencing the entire park to finally declare Haleakala goat-free. The last time I visited the park and hiked through the crater I could see the return of the mamane, the ahinahina, and many other native plants. Those unique flowering plants are bound to help increase the populations of rare and endangered Hawai'ian birds and insects that frequent them.

Pigs, Eucalyptus, and Koa Trees

Just outside the park boundary on the Kaupo side was a grove of native koa. These were trees that Hawai'ians used for canoe hulls, food containers, and a hundred other uses, and they were disappearing fast from the Maui ecosystem. Many were replaced in an experiment by Hawai'i's first territorial forester, a man named Ralph S. Hosmer. Mr. Hosmer believed in replacing native forest trees with exotic or alien species that he believed would be superior in holding water in the soils and other beneficial purposes.

It didn't work. The result of this early 20th century ecosystem tinkering was a disaster for native plants. A grove of the eucalyptus planted in Haleakala National Park is named after Mr. Hosmer and is a living example of the tinkering that has caused the extinction of so many native plants and birds in the Hawai'ian Islands.

In recent years, another alien plant, the strawberry guava, has invaded one of the last good koa groves on the East Maui Mountains. Wesley Wong, then state forester for Maui, kept hoping the koa would flourish, but feral pigs, hybridized with the pigs Hawai'ians brought when they originally discovered the islands, carried the seeds of the guava trees and the koa was threatened.

So Wes and I hunted the pigs, hoping to make some impact. We would drive a jeep up on the Kaupo Ranch, and then hike up the mountain several thousand feet and hunt. The pigs are tough. The boars carry razor-sharp tusks that can rip a hunter's leg open. Many local hunters used dogs that are trained to grab the pig's ears and pull them down for the hunter to kill. But we used no dogs, and shooting a pig that is running fast and low is not easy. But we succeeded in thinning the population for a while.

After killing the pigs we'd bone the meat from them, bag it, and pack it back down to the jeep where there was an ice chest. One night I showed up at home at a late hour with a big pack of pork, stuck it in the refrigerator, went to bed, and dreamed of Portuguese sausages. The following work day, my crew all knew that I had had a successful pig hunt and during the day I was visited by three of the work crew. Each of them closed the office door behind them and gave me a recipe card for sausage accompanied by a whispered request of "This is my family's recipe. Don't show it to anyone else." At the end of the day, I secreted the cards in my pocket and headed home.

That evening Susie and the kids and I ran all the pork and some purchased fat, used to make up for the leanest pork you ever saw, through a hand grinder, mixed them with ingredients listed on the recipe cards and stuffed casings until 1:30 in the morning.

The pork sausage was delicious, and when I served it at a park potluck, the fellows who had given me the recipes nodded secret nods at me and I winked at each in return. No one asked which recipe I had used, and I've kept the secret until now. All three recipes were the same. I suppose all of these guys were related in some way to the person who brought the recipe from Portugal in the first place.

Those park employee potluck suppers were international culinary events. Japanese-American employees brought excellent sushi. Some of the wranglers brought spicy soft jerked goat meat that they heated over charcoal. Poi and local fruits were brought by Hawai'ians and *haole* seasonal employees would bring huge tubs of Kentucky Fried Chicken. I even discovered that the work crew once hired a temporary employee of Spanish origin because his mom made the best blood sausage on Maui. The suppers were usually topped off with Adele Fevella's cake. With that cake, filled with cream and gelled fruit fillings, you practically needed to have your cardiologist's phone number readily available if you decided to have dessert.

And then when the food was gone, it was time for beer, coffee, music, some hula, and just a general good time. When I hear people complain about immigrant culture watering down America, I know that person has never been to a rural Hawai'ian potluck.

The Rain and Snow

One side of Haleakala Crater is desert. Just a few miles across the crater is one of the wettest places in the world. For a while, a 23-inch rain gauge at the Paliku Ranger cabin was checked every week by the patrol rangers. They once reported it to be overflowing after just seven days, so we had two of the big tubes used to measure the rain joined together and a wet week later the ranger discovered that it had rained more than 46 inches during one week. The upper Kipahulu valley areas above the crater were probably even wetter. They are nearly inaccessible and they contain many rare and endangered plants and birds.

People are surprised when they see pictures of snow at Haleakala. At 10,000 feet above the sea, visitors are no longer basking in the tropical warmth of the Kaanapali and Kihei beaches. The trade winds drop their moisture when they hit these high islands. In winter, a heavy wind can plaster the upper reaches of the park with a coating of ice. When there's a snowfall reported up there, local kids cut school and drive up for some winter recreation and often their first view of snow.

Cars, driven by people who have never driven on ice, go shooting off into the volcanic rock and the tow truck guy gets a lot of business. Rangers sometimes close the road when it becomes too dangerous. Then eager youngsters, often shod with flip-flops, take off running up the hill to get to the snow. It is generally a brief and jarring encounter and a few sliders require first aid for abrasions caused when they slide from the snow onto the rocks.

Po'ouli

Hawai'ian forest birds cannot live at the lower elevations. Mosquitoes, introduced to Hawai'i by whalers who dumped spoiled water into the water system on Maui, can carry the deadly parasite that causes malaria in birds. So the only living honeycreepers survive in the forests in elevations beyond the mosquito's range. The national parks and state wildlife preserves are the only protected refuges for these extremely rare birds.

In the 1970s, above the rainy area on the slopes of the mountain, a new bird was discovered. An observant University of Hawai'i undergraduate named Betsy Harrison (now Gagne) spotted the little bird and recognized it as a new species. It turned out to be a new genus as well, and the tiny bird was named *po'ouli* and was proclaimed the rarest bird in the world.

The first assault on the bird came from the State of Hawai'i Department of Fish and Game and the US Fish and Wildlife Service. They came to me asking for a permit to "take" (science talk for "kill") some birds and send them to the American Museum of Natural History in New York for determination (science for "measuring it, naming it, and stuffing it").

I was leery. In the back of my mind was the incident during the 1960s when a graduate student cut down a bristlecone pine tree to count the rings and when he had counted nearly five thousand rings, he realized that he had killed what might have been the oldest living thing on the planet. Then there were the Guadalupe fur seals, considered extinct after they had been hunted down for their fur. In 1928 an expedition found several living near sea caves in the Guadalupe Islands off Mexico. Two of the remaining few were captured and given to the San Diego Zoo. Fortunately, the other fur seals avoided more "take" and are back up to three or four thousand in number.

The upshot of this was that I refused to issue the permit for taking firearms into the area to shoot the birds. I argued that they were critically endangered birds and should be studied in the wild and when one of the birds dropped dead, then they could be taken and examined. Just think of all we'd know about the birds by then. State officials, however, said that the birds were not covered under the Endangered Species Act because they were not yet a species. With that puzzling non-rationale, the biologists happily helicoptered into an area just outside the National Park Boundary and shot some of the birds, sent them to the East Coast of the mainland and had them determined, named, and stuffed.

Since 2006 the po'ouli has not been seen and is suspected of being extinct. The population dwindled down from an estimated 200 birds to likely three, and one of those died in captivity. The culprit suspected in the disappearance is the mountain pig, a hybrid of the pigs Hawai'ians brought to these islands during the first millennium AD and domestic farm pigs that escaped from captivity and interbred. Like the goats, the pigs destroy the native habitat and carry the seeds of exotic plants, which aggressively take over. The State of Hawai'i and The Nature Conservancy put together a refuge for the po'ouli but it seemed it was too little, too late. Before they could get an effective fence to exclude the pigs, the habitat was altered and the tiny birds, the rarest in the world, have most likely followed the dozens of Hawai'ian birds that have gone down the one-way road to extinction.

Not a Paniolo

The Mexican cowboys brought to Maui and other islands in the 1800s to work the cattle on the Ulupalakua, Haleakala, and other big ranches were known as *paniolos*, a Hawai'ian corruption of *espaniola* or Spanish. The Hawai'ians took to horsemanship quickly and in 1910 three local Maui cowboys took three high places in the world championship rodeo in Cheyenne, Wyoming. In that competition, Ikua Purdy was first in steer roping. The Purdy men were not the only good riders. Aunty Harriet Purdy was one of the people who rode horses that jumped off the steel pier in Atlantic City, entertaining thousands of thrill seekers. The Hawai'ians learned to break their horses by riding them in belly-deep saltwater. The horse couldn't get enough traction to buck the rider off and the cowboys were able to train the horse without a lot of abuse.

When I got to my job on Maui, I was a mediocre rider. I had ridden horse patrol in Yosemite a few times and had packed and ridden mules at the training center at Grand Canyon, but I wasn't very good at horsemanship. My crew, on the other hand, had been packing and riding in the crater for many years and were expert horsemen. They would take a pack string into the back country, delivering firewood to the three cabins and maintaining trails and shelters.

Following my mentor Bob Howe's advice, I hiked through the crater at least once a month during my years as superintendent. But the time came when I decided to ride with the work crew. The horse I was assigned was huge. They told me he was half thoroughbred and half work horse, and they could have been kidding, but it didn't appear so.

We rode to the trail head and started down the narrow cliff side switchbacks into the crater. The trail had been blasted out of sheer rock by the Civilian Conservation Corps in the 1930s and was kept in excellent condition by the crew. Mules carried packs of gravel that could be dumped by yanking on a cord, a primitive and effective dump truck for a wilderness where vehicles were not allowed. The dropoff from the trail was sheer, but the horses knew what they were doing and I was instructed to keep loose reins on the way down because, according to one of the wranglers, "After all, boss, da horse no like fall off da cliff either."

We off loaded the firewood and continued across the crater floor. It was a gorgeous Maui day and I was feeling pretty good about it all, but of course, it didn't last. While traversing an area of coarse lava, something spooked my horse. It may have been one of the nene geese in the area around Kapalaoa or something wholly in my horse's imagination, but he started to run and buck. It would have taken one of the famous Purdy family members to stay on and I wasn't one of them. I went airborne and landed in a patch of that coarse lava.

None of my bones were broken, but I had landed on my hands and knees and my knees were bloodied and my palms had about fifty small pieces of sharp bits of lava stuck in them. If this had been a western movie I'd have remounted and tamed the horse. It wasn't. I walked on to the ranger cabin at Paliku and spent the evening picking bits of lava out of my hands and knees and swabbing the wounds in alcohol. I walked out the next day and decided that the horse was not in my future for trips into the crater. All of my subsequent trips through Haleakala were on what the old cowboys called "shank's mare" — on foot.

Kanaha Pond

To be honest, these ponds at Kanaha were not spectacular. They were natural wetlands that were enhanced by early Hawai'ian people for fish production. The ponds were situated near one of the busiest airports in Hawai'i and had some light industrial neighbors. Great numbers of rental cars and commercial traffic buzzed by on one side, and the remnants of World War II defense emplacements were still there on the beachside in 1972. Hawai'ian stilts, coots, and ducks hang out there, dipping up their lunch from the tiny plants and critters that live in these ponds. The thing that made it special was that many of the birds were listed on the US Endangered Species Register. Herons and other birds used the ponds as well.

The ponds are fed by a freshwater lens that exists under the island of Maui. Rain falls in great quantities on the windward sides of these islands. The rainfall percolates down through the porous volcanic soils and creates a huge lens of fresh water beneath the island. Excess fresh water leaks out into the saltwater and can be seen and felt when snorkeling around the rocky shore. It is colder than the surrounding warm saltwater.

Enter into this idyllic scene the County of Maui water treatment plant. The county had a couple of choices of where to build the sewer treatment plant and where to pump the treated water. They chose Kanaha Pond. The plan was to pump the secondary treated water deep under the pond and it would supposedly stay there for a few years and everything would be okay. Wait a minute! What's the temperature of that water? Oh yes, that's several degrees warmer than the cold fresh water at the bottom. What makes you think that nutrient-rich soup down there will not rise immediately to the surface and fertilize the ambient surface water, creating another big green scum pond?

Prior to this proposal, I had been elected president of the Maui chapter of The Conservation Council for Hawai'i, and I decided to challenge the county. You can't really separate your work-self from your protest-self in these situations, so the mayor of Maui County called in some political chips in the person of Sam Prior, an aging retired Pan Am Airlines executive and aviation pioneer who lived in Kipahulu.

Locally, Sam was famous for having a federal narcotics agent badge that someone in the Nixon administration had given him. He carried a semi-automatic pistol under his aloha shirts and threatened to arrest the hippies who smoked dope and ingested magic mushrooms that had the bad manners to grow in the national park near the ocean. Harry Hasegawa, the general store proprietor in Hana, is supposed to have told Sam he would be banned from shopping there if he didn't stop carrying the pistol in his store. The alternative to shopping at Hasegawa's General Store was a four-hour round trip drive to the nearest market. This wasn't a classic Second Amendment issue. Sam had dropped the pistol on the floor when he was reaching for something on the bottom shelf and Harry was afraid it might go off and shoot one of the other octogenarians who shopped there.

Back to the pond. It turns out that the mayor knew that Sam's nephew, Nathanial Prior Reed, was the Assistant

Secretary of the Interior for Fish, Wildlife, and Parks. So the mayor called Sam and Sam called his nephew and asked to have me either removed or at least stifled. I got a phone call from Nat Reed and was questioned about the dispute. I filled him in as best I could and he told me I was doing the right thing and not to worry about his uncle.

The newly formed Environmental Protection Agency (EPA) was preparing to approve the project. Our local conservation council was relatively powerless, and so I called the National Wildlife Federation in Washington, DC, for help. When they found out what was at stake, they sent a young attorney out and he helped us fight off the project. Injecting secondary treated sewage into the water supply of the island seems foolish, but it's what was recommended by EPA in the 1970s and the county went ahead and did it at several locations. We were able to hold them off at Kanaha, but in the other areas the cost has been coming due. Water is seeping out onto reefs and forming algae that can destroy them. Lawsuits have continued to fly and all could have been solved by charging all the newly constructed buildings the costs of full treatment so the water could be reused anywhere on the island. If there is anything I hate, it's having to say, "I told you so."

CHAPTER 20

Rainbow Bridge and the Convergence

It was the 1970s and the Haight-Ashbury community had followed me from Yosemite to Maui. Flower children were everywhere on Maui. Conflict reigned in the community where local folks got very uptight about youngsters with a different lifestyle and a willingness to enter on private property and pick the family papayas as they strolled by. The Haleakala Crater, not surprisingly, had gotten a reputation as a spiritual force center. Jimi Hendrix came to Maui, performed his last American concert, and made a movie called *Rainbow Bridge* in which he traveled to the spiritual center of the crater to play music.

Conflict between staff and the flock of "new lifestyle" people caused a lot of grief because many of the park employees were from the local Maui population. And during the 1970s, Maui was not the laidback picture often portrayed in the media; many folks there were religious and socially conservative. I had to counsel some employees about the civil rights enjoyed by all folks and one employee quit over such conflicts.

The chief ranger was not fond of the flower children, which was obvious with his obsessive observations about body odor and general cleanliness. In general, visitors were allowed to use the telephone at the information desk to make local calls, but if the chief saw a hippie using the phone, he'd stroll out with a can of Lysol disinfectant and spray the mouthpiece in front of the person who had just finished their call. Adele Fevella, the receptionist, came into my office one day and told me the telephone wasn't working. I went out and unscrewed the mouthpiece on the receiver, and discovered that the entire inside of the telephone transmitter had turned to plastic goo. The chief ranger had sprayed so much Lysol in it that it had melted the insides. I counseled the chief about the dangers of overuse of Lysol.

Later, in the late 1980s, thousands of New Age proponents and some Hawai'ians gathered in the crater to experience the harmonic convergence of planets in our solar system. Haleakala has always had spiritual significance, and the visits of those trying to connect with something spiritual continue to this day. It seems like an American version of the pilgrimages of Europe and the Middle East. And speaking of the unknown...

Death Lights

Dope smoking was pretty common on Maui during the 1970s and some people used all manner of hallucinogens to excess. One young man had ingested some unknown drug along the shore in Kipahulu and suffered a serious freakout event requiring hospitalization. He claimed he had seen the "will o' the wisp" lights at Kipahulu, lights that in local lore were supposed to portend someone's death. On the day after his hospitalization, I got a call from Charles Lindbergh, saying that he and Sam Prior had been having a glass of wine on Sam's porch and they had also seen the eerie floating lights go by.

The "death" lights quickly became a serious topic of conversation around Hana. I was driving through the rural area west of Hana one evening soon thereafter and the shifting lights appeared off to one side. I had the heebee-jeebees, but I figured if the lights were going to get me anyway, I might as well have a good look. I took the next turn and there before me in a small fenced pasture sat about thirty Hawai'ians watching some program on a small black and white portable TV plugged into a long extension cord. *These* were my "death lights"! I got out of the car to see what was going on and was handed a Primo beer and a folding chair while we watched some TV show. This pasture was the only location in the neighborhood where the TV signal could be captured. I can't say whether the "death" lights are real. If they are, either I must not have seen them or they aren't specific about when you are going to die: just that you will at some point.

Bureaucracy: The Bear Damage Report

Automated reporting had come to the National Park Service. Each national park was supposed to file a "bear damage report" every year so someone in some office in San Francisco could compile the statistics and forward them to some other person in Washington, DC.

Then, one can assume, they would be included in an annual report that hardly anyone would read. Don't get me wrong. There are good reasons to know about these things. The trouble is that the closest bear was in the Honolulu Zoo and to have bear damage occur in Haleakala required that a bear escape from the zoo, cross the Koolau Mountains and several busy highways, swim the 41 miles across the nasty Kaiwi channel, and then get past some of my relatives on Molokai who would likely shoot the bear and cook it in a ground oven and have a hell of a big luau. If the bear got past that and then swam across the Pailolo Channel with its big winds, and if it was still able to walk, climb the mountain, *and* cause some damage, then I would file the report.

I tossed the reports, when they came, in the wastebasket for two years but kept getting annoying automated reminder letters asking why the report was late. The solution to the problem came when I received a report from Tom Vaughn that a pet gibbon owned by Sam Prior had bitten a park visitor when the person tried to pet the animal. Seizing on this incident, Tom and I cobbled together an "Ape Damage Report" and sent it along to the regional office. Months later, on a trip to San Francisco for a meeting, I sneaked into the office of the person assigned to the reports and found the ape report in his "hold basket," the one where you put things you have no idea what to do with. The good news was that we stopped getting the request to count Hawai'ian bear damage.

In Which I Become a Rotarian

My supervisor Bob Barrel was one of my favorite people. He had a small office in Honolulu and was charged with supervising those of us who ran the national parks in Hawai'i. Bob was the liaison with state and federal offices. When I was given my initial assignments, Bob added, "You need to join the Maui Rotary Club." I had previously been taken as a guest to the meeting at the Maui Country Club at Spreckelsville. The place was named for Claus Spreckels, the German entrepreneur who had bamboozled the king into dividing up the land in favor of the sugar planters and ending the Hawai'ian land system that had sufficed for more than a millennium. Me join the Maui Rotary? I protested. The Maui club only had one Hawai'ian and two part Hawai'ians on its rolls. The only representative of the big Asian-American community was the beer distributor who had the same social status I did. The Hawai'ian was Reverend John Kukahiko, a preacher who would pray in Hawai'ian before the white members of this all-male club sat down for their weekly lunch.

I protested. The Kahului Rotary Club, just down the road, was where the non-white and newcomers met, and that was the club I was more inclined to join. But Bob insisted. "The Maui Rotary is where the power structure meets, and you need to know them and what they are doing," he said. "If you don't like what they are doing, then change them." So I joined.

I volunteered for the job no one wanted, program chairman. So I arranged for the old-guard descendants of the missionaries, plantation owners, and real estate barons along with the professional doctors and lawyers to be treated to weekly talks from feminists and Hawai'ian activists among the usual rubber-chicken circuit speakers, and resolutions were presented to allow women into Rotary and other "radical" actions. One of Rotary International's four-way tests for actions is, "Is it fair to all concerned?" Today, there is more diversity and women are members. The pressure from members in the 1970s helped make Rotary more relevant. Some of the members recognized the need for change and I found some good friends among them. Today, women are welcome in Rotary.

CHAPTER 21

People

In 1973, my friend John Bose was writing a column for a local paper, and asked to join me on a trip to Molokai where a meeting of the Aboriginal Lands of Hawai'ian Ancestry (ALOHA) Association was taking place. I was unable to be a voting member because of my position as manager of substantial federal lands. But like many beginning organizations the association was spending a lot of time arguing over penny-ante monetary issues instead of discussing potential land claims. I volunteered to be the treasurer and straightened out the books.

John attended the meeting as a journalist, and after the meetings were finished, I took him to Pukoo to see where my family had come from. One of my grandmother's brothers still lived in the old house and invited us in for a cold drink. Uncle Jack was a throw-net fisherman, and his walls were decorated with items he had found while fishing. One unusual glass float caught John's eye and he said, "Oh! I really like that one." Uncle Jack immediately took the float off its perch and handed it to John. "Here," he said. "Take this with you." John replied, "I can't take this." And then a discussion ensued between them with Uncle Jack insisting and John trying to give it back.

The result of this was that John took the float home and wrote a column advising people not to admire things in the houses of Native Hawai'ians. Saying you "like" something is tantamount to saying you want it. Hawai'ians, particularly those old timers raised in rural Hawai'i, will insist that you take it with you. Their innate generosity reminds me of American Indians. North American natives helped early immigrants to survive and were rewarded with the loss of their lands, their livelihoods and, in many cases, their lives. They guided the vanguard of Euro-Americans across the continent and again were killed and/or rounded up onto reservations. Similarly, in Hawai'i the people lost their land and most of their culture. These days, young Hawai'ians are making serious attempts to regain some of what was lost. But the population of Hawai'ians, now down to about 10% in their own islands, has an uphill battle ahead. It is my hope that the tradition of militancy can go hand-in-hand with the tradition of generosity.

On leaving Molokai, Uncle Jack handed me a hind quarter of a deer wrapped in freezer paper. I asked when he had shot it. "Oh no," he said, with a big grin. "Da buggah ran down from da hill, Sistah opened da freezer and da buggah jump right in." So when my luggage came down the ramp at the Maui airport, amidst much Hawai'ian hilarity, it was accompanied by a frozen leg of venison that may or may not have been shot during hunting season.

My fondest memory of Hawai'ian generosity is of a drive I took around the unpaved portion of East Maui. At one point in the graveled road there was a one-way stretch that wove down into a deep gulch and back up the other side. Cars and trucks couldn't pass, so you looked down to see if anyone was coming, and when you saw the dust cloud you waited your turn. On the day in question I was returning the back way from Kipahulu. I looked down and saw that an old truck, traveling very slowly, had started down the opposite side. I was stuck in the heat with nothing to do but wait. After what seemed like an hour, but was probably ten minutes, the old truck crawled up the hill and as it passed, an elderly Hawai'ian man reached out and handed me a can of beer from a cooler sitting next to him on the seat. He said nothing and drove on. Sitting in a government car in uniform on a blazing hot day, I considered the propriety of the situation, cracked open the beer and sucked down the coldest and best beer I can ever remember drinking.

Frank Freitas

For many years, Frank Freitas had been guiding people on horseback down into Haleakala Crater. He supplied the horses and did the cooking for the overnight stays. Frank was a loud old man with a hundred tales to tell. Some of them were true but all were most entertaining. He would show up at my house at the oddest times. One Easter he came into my house, sat down at the dinner table and asked to eat dinner with us because the children in his family gathering wouldn't turn off the TV and, according to Frank, all that was on was mentally ill people making fools of themselves. Susie obligingly set another plate and Frank shouted, "Good bread, good meat, good God, let's eat!" And he dug in.

On a day we were building holding pens to keep the children's 4-H steers from galloping off, Frank showed up with his tools and taught the kids how to work with eucalyptus, a very hard wood that grew on our place. If you had some difficult work to do, old Frank's truck would pull up and he'd pitch in. If you had something particularly good to eat, he'd show up for that too. He was a great camp cook, and when the staff at the park held potluck suppers, Frank would arrive with a three-gallon container of some spicy chicken stew or some other specialty, and he would get in the chow line with one of those big Army stainless steel food trays and load up.

One of the wranglers who worked for me advised me to go to Makawao and watch Frank train horses. It was an experience I will not forget. Frank Freitas chose the horses when they were just colts weaned from the mare. He gentled them from day one. When they became yearlings, he'd tie stuff on them in different ways, and hang out while they got used to the burdens, all the while talking and gentling them. Before the horses were ever taken on trail rides, he had the young horses spending days in the corral with full packs on. He even tied yellow raincoats onto them and let the wind flap it all over the place until they were used to the disturbance. When I knew the old man, he was getting on in years and he had trained the horse he rode to walk up a ramp into the tack room and stand next to his saddle rack so he could get the saddle onto the horses back without having to lift or carry it. Then the horse would back down the ramp. I heard Frank yell on many occasions, but never at his horses.

Richard Marks

The Kalaupapa Peninsula sticks out from the base of the cliffs on windward Molokai. Access is difficult. Today, you can visit via small aircraft that sometimes have to time their takeoff and landing runs to avoid huge blasts of saltwater blowing up from waves crashing into the end of the short airstrip. Or you can come into windward Molokai on a boat and negotiate around some rocks into the landing at Kalawao. Some boats have gone aground and wrecked on the rocks. The third access is via mule train or on foot down one of the steepest trails in Hawai'i.

The difficult access is why the peninsula became a leper's colony. Hansen's disease, commonly called leprosy, is an age-old scourge. You can read of lepers in the Bible. In Leviticus 13, the blueprint for the isolation of lepers is made clear. Priests would examine people with lesions or serious rashes and if the sores persisted for two weeks, the people were labeled as unclean and isolated outside the village. Modern science will tell you that the disease is transmitted by a bacterium in the same genus as the one causing tuberculosis. It is treatable with drugs and cannot be transmitted once the treatment takes hold. But the damage to faces, hands, feet, and other tissues is irreversible. The few cases popping up in the US today are from people who contracted the disease in another country.

In 1865, King Lot Kamehameha ordered the removal of a community that had existed on the peninsula for 900 or so years. Lepers were declared legally dead, transported to Kalawao, and dumped off to survive on their own. During the 1870s, Catholic priests and nuns came to Kalaupapa and helped to bring order to the chaos that existed at the colony. Josef De Veuster, a Belgian priest known as Father Damien, is the best known of these. He himself contracted the disease and died in 1889. For his work with the lepers, he was canonized by the Catholic Church. An excellent source to learn more about this unique piece of Hawai'ian history is the book *Holy Man* by Gavan Daws.

On a trip to Molokai, I was approached by Richard Marks, a man with Hansen's disease. Like his parents, Richard had contracted the disease and was a resident at Kalaupapa. He lived with his wife, Gloria, another of the few survivors of the disease who remained at the colony and received treatment from State of Hawai'i healthcare providers. Richard ran Damien Tours, a one-person business consisting of an old van that he had fashioned into a transport for the few tourists who got permission to visit. The vehicle had an awning with a fringe on top and benches in the back for the tourists.

Richard was afraid that when the last patient died, the governments of the State and County would turn Kalaupapa into another big tourist destination with expensive hotels and condominiums. His worry was well founded. He had approached Patsy Mink, a member of Congress from Hawai'i, about making Kalaupapa into a national historical park, and he needed some help. I had two irons in this fire. One was I agreed with Richard's assessment of the likely outcome if the land was left to the State and County, and the other was family history. Two of my grandmother's teenaged sisters, infected with Hansen's disease, were sent to Kalaupapa and are buried there.

Thus began an association with Richard that included many hikes to the colony and sessions on into the night where we drafted the elements of a bill to bring Kalaupapa into the National Park System. Representative Mink had the bill properly written and introduced. The legislative liaison office of the Park Service in Washington, DC, sent the bill to me for comments. I was able to give it high marks. The current existence of this important part of our history is owed, largely, to the late Richard Marks and his persistence and to the late Patsy Takemoto Mink, a hard-working and effective member of the US Congress. As an aside, my youngest sister recently served a couple of six-month tours of duty as an archeologist at Kalaupapa and located the burial places of our two great aunts.

The Whole Earth Movement

During our time in Hawai'i, Susie and I had become enamored with the Whole Earth movement. We raised chickens, geese, and rabbits and had a big garden. Susie converted the front lawn into a taro patch, obtained hulis or starts from State Forester Wesley Wong's father, and grew fifteen or so varieties of taro in our yard. Many Hawai'ian people came by the house to get starts from her plants, some of which were quite rare. On weekends we would load the kids in the car and drive to remote areas to fish and gather the wild foods that were abundant in public areas. Hawai'ian mountain apples, mangos, avocados, coconuts, and many other foods could be had for the picking. I climbed to remote mountains above Kaupo and hunted wild pigs and goats.

A neighbor and I fished a short gill net out of a truck inner tube we would paddle and push out between a couple of reefs. We'd leave the net for a couple of hours and come back for it. We caught eight or ten different kinds of fish, which we would wrap in foil with coconut milk and roast in the imu fire pit in our backyard. I spent time repairing the net after an occasional shark or a group of bonefish would trash it. When Micronesian students at the Mauna Olu campus of United States International University found out about us, we'd have frequent visits from them. They were not thriving on American cafeteria food, and they taught me how to prepare the reef fish to eliminate its strong odor and helped cook it on the hot stones, turning it into a delicious meal we could share.

My two oldest children got to participate in the summer school program of Kamehameha Schools and came home with some idea of the culture they were part of. And my youngest child, Matt, became a fantastic scrounger, locating old dumps that contained historical bottles and other treasures. The children raised 4-H animals, played music in school bands, and participated in sports at the elementary and middle schools.

Susie led groups of Girl Scouts and other children on hikes into the crater and gave classes on the natural history of Maui. She also created some wonderful paintings using watercolors, oils, and acrylics.

CHAPTER 22

Back to Alaska

In the winter of 1973, I flew to Alaska and bought a piece of remote forested land in Gustavus. It was five or six miles from the headquarters of Glacier Bay National Park. Eugene Chase, the homesteader, had patented the land under the Homestead Act and was selling off a couple of 20-acre parcels. Susie and I planned to build a retirement cabin in the woods at some future time.

The concept of building our own place using our own hands and as much local material as possible was our dream. We didn't realize how close that future was to be. The children were aged ten, twelve, and fourteen when we decided the time was right for an adventure. The Park Service had been good to us, but the 1970s were calling with a song that said, "Bust out of your routine and try something difficult." I resigned from the National Park Service. We said our good-byes to some good friends in Hawai'i, sold the house and the furniture, packed a plywood crate with our tools and essentials and headed north to Alaska.

In May 1973 we pitched a mountain tent in a clearing on the land in Gustavus and started building our cabin. My father had dreamed of building his own home, and during my childhood I had helped with construction of two major additions to homes during the period when our family was growing. Dad had given me a book that I had kept in mind all these years, titled *Your Dream Home and How to Build It for Less Than $3,500* by Hubbard Cobb. The book was dated in respect to the dollars needed, but it included plans for a vacation cabin of about 600 square feet. My friend Steve Steinhour found a canvas supplier in Colorado who made a fourteen- by sixteen-foot wall tent and shipped it to us. The woods construction camp had begun.

It was spring in Alaska and the days were long. At mid-summer the sun would drop down below the horizon at 10 p.m. and pop up at 3:30 a.m. In between those hours was a twilight. It made for long work days. Vegetables, responding to the long hours of light, grew like crazy.

We built a tent frame with lodgepole pine stems and fitted the tent to it with an outside ridge pole and a complete canvas fly over the whole thing. We fashioned a floor, a sleeping platform, and cut a hole for a stovepipe with its insulated fitting. Inside was a sheepherder's stove that swallowed firewood like an old steam locomotive. We were fortunate to have a bounty of already dry firewood from pine trees that were dying out as the forest matured and spruce and hemlocks replaced the pine. All food was prepared on a little shelf and cooked on the iron stove top and we ate, read, and conversed while seated on the edge of the sleeping platform.

Susie crafted a set of drawings adapted from the plans in the book and I drew a framing plan that used as many natural logs as possible. When we were satisfied with the plans, I flew to Juneau and bought an old Chevy pickup, bought supplies, lumber, nails, chimney fittings, and some materials I had scrounged from the collapsed structure at the A.J. Mine, and loaded it onto a barge bound for Gustavus. I hitched a ride on a fishing boat and headed the sixty-five miles west to meet the barge.

A friend lent us a flat-bed trailer and we hauled the loads out into the woods. Most of the materials were carried 300 feet from the road by hand or on a cart we had purchased. We had decided to forgo a generator, and so the construction began with a chainsaw as our only power tool. In my absence, Susie and the children had done a lot of clearing of brush and small trees, so I pitched in for the heavy digging and we cleared the cabin site and a large garden spot where Susie planted crops of potatoes, onions, and many green vegetables.

The building site was wet at the time we constructed the cabin. The land that had been covered by glaciers only 200 years before was undergoing a process called isostatic rebound. In simple terms, it was rising about an inch a year. But the water table on our land was pretty high at the time. Digging on the house site, we found water only about a foot down from the surface.

So instead of a concrete foundation, we found some damaged creosote pilings at a local dump and I salvaged sections and set them in as rows of pilings.

After getting the tops level, we cut three 40-foot logs, dragged them to the house site, and enlisted as many local folks as we could to help us roll the logs up ramps onto the pilings and spike them down. The floor joists went across the logs and a plywood floor was laid down. Log columns and beams were axed out of some dried spruce, pine, and hemlock logs and the framing went up to fill in the remainder of the structure. We fashioned big mortice and tenon joints and pinned them with pieces of steel rebar.

During the construction we had to deal with a large black bear. Right across our property was a regular bear highway, with their footprints beaten into the moss. Most bears stayed away from us, but one had to be dealt with. Fresh food was kept in a big truck toolbox we had salvaged. Other food supplies were stacked in boxes on a pallet and enclosed with plywood from a shipping container. The adventurous black bear managed to rip the top of the steel box open, leaving some hair and a little blood on the open case. We realized we were invading his territory and tried to be philosophical about it. But we reached the end of our patience when the bear decided to crawl under the building structure and started chewing on the windows that were still in their cardboard boxes.

The windows were the expensive part of our purchase and we didn't have the funds for replacing them, so I figured the bear would have to go. I tried shooting off the shotgun in his direction, but it didn't faze him. So we decided to kill him and got out the pressure canner to preserve some bear meat for the winter. I loaded a rifled slug into the twelve gauge and took aim at what I could see of the bear—his head—and pulled the trigger. *Boom!* went the shotgun. Up came the startled bear's head and smashed into the log he had crawled under. He crawled out and took off zigzagging through the woods.

I was mortified that I had only wounded the bear. I got my 30-30 Winchester and with Tim toting the shotgun, we started tracking the bear. All we found were smashed bushes where the big fellow had run straight through the underbrush on his way to wherever angry bears go. I kept an eye behind us, knowing that bears will sometimes circle and check you out from behind, but this bear was headed out, and we found no blood sign. After an hour or so of tracking, we returned to the cabin site.

When I crawled under the structure, I found that the slug had struck the bottom of a log an inch or so over the bear's head and bounced down, probably ricocheting off the bear's skull but not doing more than giving him an instant and massive headache. We never saw that bear again. I hiked several times looking for a carcass and sniffing for evidence of a dead bear but never found one. For all we know, he may still be running, and the good news was that we didn't have to stop construction. Since that day, more than forty years have passed with no bear incidents at the cabin. We are very careful with garbage, and the bears that graze by the cabin eating cranberries and blueberries either leave when they hear us or just ignore us.

Construction went on, but on the rare day when the temperature hit 70 degrees, we'd put the tools down and hike to the river for a fast skinny dip in the cold stream. On one of those days we spotted a pile of brush that looked out of place and I looked inside. There was a crate under the brush, and when we uncovered it, we found a huge eight-foot, half-round piece of glass inside. I asked around and found out that the glass had been ordered by Glacier Bay Lodge, to cover the opening of the two-sided fireplace that was on the side where the bar was. The manager had a fear of drunks fighting and falling into the fire.

It turned out that the glass had been ordered an inch too small and was left at the park dump for a few years, where it was discovered by some hippies who intended to use it to make a sauna next to the river. They got permission to take it, and then, as is often the case, they never got around to it and the window had lain there for another year. The whole thing weighed 200 pounds and was three-eighths of an inch thick tempered safety plate glass. I asked around and no one claimed it, so I managed to get the pickup down to the river and we took it home and carried it through the woods. Using some driftwood planks, I framed the thing and installed it in the front of the cabin. To this day it is the focal point of the place, looking south and seeing moose, bears, and other animals passing by.

I had pledged to build the cabin without power tools, but when we had nailed the siding on and had the roof shingled, I had to cut out the plywood covering the window frames. It was late November and the weather had turned. The rain that had pooled on the flooring of the cabin had turned to ice, and it was time to get the heck out of the tent and into more permanent housing. I fired up the chainsaw and carved out the plywood in the window frames. Within three days I had the windows in and closed up the door opening while I built a door. We installed our cook stove, hooked up the chimney, and fired it up, turning the interior into a giant steam bath while the water was driven out of the structure.

On December fourth we moved from the tent into the cabin. Over the past forty-plus years I have been putting the finishing touches on the cabin. I assume it's like the Winchester Mystery House and if I ever finish it I will drop dead. Who knows?

A Year in the Woods

Winter showed up on time, and we got insulation up on the inside of the cabin and finally drove the moisture out of the place. After four months in the tent, the cabin seemed palatial in contrast. We had driven a sand point well next to the garden, a good distance from the outhouse, and pumped water by hand, carrying it to the cabin in buckets. A big boiler pot on the wood stove provided hot water and we all became adept at cooking on that stove. My morning duty was to get up and quickly light the wood stove and bring in fresh water for the morning washup. Meanwhile, the children were snuggled into sleeping bags until either the cabin warmed up or their bladders cried out for mercy and they bundled up and raced to the outhouse. As for Susie, she wouldn't budge until a cup of coffee was proffered at the entrance to the pile of quilts she hid under.

Once the children were off to school, involving a half-mile walk to the road and a ride from Mrs. Lesh and her VW bus/school bus, we'd begin the day's chores, work on the cabin, woodcutting and splitting, and food gathering. My shotgun got us ducks from around the Good River where I would hunt with my friend Larry Tong, and I'd get a deer once in a while by taking the canoe to Pleasant Island, a mile or so across Icy Passage. One neighbor gave us some canned bear meat, which was like beef pot roast. But we also ate canned Spam and canned corned beef on occasion. Vegetables and fruit were hard to come by in winter and we ordered freeze-dried fruit and vegetables from an organic food shipper and ate fairly healthy meals, although the dried vegetables made us dream at night about fresh produce.

The children did well in the one-room school at Gustavus. The two younger ones, Matt and Joan, attended and got a good start on their education from Pat Fitzgerald, the teacher for grades one through eight. Susie volunteered to teach art and I taught music and had a great group of kids singing Hawai'ian songs and other music during their holiday celebration.

Tim was in the ninth grade and because there was no high school, he took correspondence courses taught by student teachers and their professors at the University of Nebraska. He decided to learn to play the baritone horn, and so the Alaska high school coordinator found one we could afford at a pawn shop in Ketchikan and shipped it out. We repaired it with duct tape and Tim would sit on a stump and play the mellow sounds into a small tape player. We'd mail the tape to Nebraska and he'd go on with the lessons. Then a tape would come back from his remote instructor, who gave advice on how to improve. This may sound bizarre, but it worked. Tim became a fine baritone and French horn player, studied music in college, and has performed in orchestras, ensembles, and bands around the country.

At the beginning of spring we picked dwarf fireweed shoots and young sour-dock leaves. They were loaded with vitamin C and were tasty as well. As soon as fish began to show up we'd get to the river for Dolly Varden char and haunt the community pier, hoping for an early salmon or any other edible fish. My children and I have caught hundreds of fish from the old pier over the years. It was our cornucopia for healthful food.

For produce, Susie had written the Agriculture Extension Service at Haines and asked for advice on varieties of different vegetables that we could grow. Their answers had more negatives than positives, but it didn't put her off. She ordered sixty or so different packets of seeds from Burpee Seeds and planted them all. To this day, I can pull her journal out of the bookcase in the cabin and read about the results from her experiments. It turned out that the ag-extension people knew a lot less about what to grow there than Susie did. The upshot was a bounty of good green vegetables and potatoes to go with the abundant wild berries, and our diet became greatly improved.

Later in spring, the king salmon would show up. One of our neighbors, Gary Owens, and my son Matt and I would fish in shallow water near the old fish trap pilings five or so miles from the river. One day, Matt hooked and played a huge salmon and handed the rod to me after ten or fifteen minutes, and after a half hour of the fight, we pulled a 44-pound shining king salmon over the canoe gunwales. The fish was so long its head went up one side of the canoe and its tail up the other side. Dave Lesh, who was fishing for the Gustavus Inn, hauled the big salmon back to the river in his boat and after divvying it up with neighbors, we ate that fantastic fish. I can still taste it.

With no refrigeration, our fishing trips tended to be brief. Catch enough to eat, take it home, and cook or smoke it and go out another day. Matt became adept at catching trout and pink salmon in the river and we ate pretty well that summer. When the coho salmon came in, we smoked fish and canned it in glass jars for the winter.

CHAPTER 23

The End of the Experiment and a New Challenge

We lasted about fourteen months. I picked up an odd job now and then, but the bank account dwindled and vanished and by fall, I needed to find work. Susie wanted to tough it out, but I was nervous about the whole deal and so hitched a ride on a boat to Juneau and went to work handling fish at Juneau Cold Storage.

The Cold Storage was on South Franklin Street about where the aerial tram station is now. Across the street was the City Café, a busy diner run by Sam Taguchi, a man with a rough personality and a great ability at the grill. Governors ate there as well as winos sipping cups of Sam's scalding black coffee. The place was loud and the food was plentiful. If there was trouble, Sam, all 120 pounds of him, would whip out from behind the counter and toss the offenders out. Police weren't needed.

I was pretty broke, but a friend, Bill Leighty, and his wife, Nancy Waterman, had a home under construction and I camped in the nearly finished building to keep the lumber from walking away. A couple of evenings each week, I'd go to the Leightys' Gold Creek Salmon

Bake outdoor restaurant and play guitar and sing for my supper and tips. There was some cash flow to send home and while the work at the Cold Storage was strenuous and healthy, it wouldn't last beyond fishing seasons when there would be no herring or salmon to freeze and ship.

Working in the Cold Storage for eight hours a day was interesting. The Salvation Army store was adjacent to the work place, and we'd buy old sweaters and wear three at a time to keep warm. Long underwear was standard clothing. A friend and I calculated that we each stacked 35,000 pounds of frozen chum salmon in a truck during one shift. Just as in my cannery days, I got very strong. I'd arm wrestle guys for beer after work and seldom had to buy.

One day I was helping an elderly fellow carry some cases of fishing nets up to the loft where he worked repairing gill nets. When he learned that I had come in from Gustavus, he pulled out his identification card. It turned out that Willis Peters was a Tlingit Indian and his tribal ID listed his birthplace as Strawberry Point, Alaska. Mr. Willis had been born in a fishing camp not far from where my cabin stood in what has now been named Gustavus. Small world indeed.

As the fishing season was winding down I started looking for other work. I saw an advertisement from Alaska State Parks. They were looking for a district park superintendent for the Chugach District in the Anchorage area. I applied and was given an interview by Guy Martin, the commissioner of natural resources for the state. I cleaned up as well as I could and showed up at his office. Guy told me later that I smelled like fish during the interview, but he was able to overlook it. After the interview, he asked me whether I'd be interested in being the director of the Alaska State Park System. The director, who had also served as state forester, was retiring and the job was coming open in a month. Governor Jay Hammond interviewed me and approved. After a consultation with Susie, I agreed and took the job. I finished up at the Cold Storage, packed a bag, and flew to Anchorage. Susie and the kids followed shortly thereafter.

A recent governor of Alaska portrayed herself as a real Alaskan; a mama grizzly. I suppose it's okay to call yourself that if you live there. But the real Alaskan governor was Jay Hammond. Jay was a muscular well-spoken guy who had married a Native Alaskan woman from the Bristol Bay area and had two lovely daughters. He is the only American governor I know of who had a degree in wildlife management. He had a homestead at Lake Clark and flew a bush plane into some pretty remote places. A centrist Republican, he held the reins of the state during the time of transition to the modern era of oil exploration. He was unpretentious and would hold his meetings with those of us stationed in Anchorage over breakfast at McDonald's. When he became frustrated with the recalcitrant legislature, he'd go home and lift weights to burn off the frustration. His natural resources person was my boss, Guy Martin, a lawyer who was charged with taking care of the state's interests during the time of the Native Claims Settlement work and the building of the oil pipeline. These men were two giants in Alaska's history and I was privileged to work for them.

Alaska State Parks

It was 1975. The park system was spread all over Central and South Central Alaska. The oil boom had not yet started and my job entailed running a system of remote wayside campgrounds, originally designed to keep down the potential for bush fires. There were a few large parks like Chugach at nearly a half million acres and Denali State Park, which often had the best views of the great mountain. Most of the park use took place in the summer, but winter recreation was popular with snowmobiling at Nancy Lake and cross-country skiing in many areas. There were also historic sites like the Totem Bight Park in Ketchikan and Fort Abercrombie on Kodiak Island. The job included running the state recreation planning and grant programs and managing the state's archeology and historic preservation programs. The total number of full-time employee (FTE) equivalents assigned to do all of this was thirty-nine. The mythical FTE can be a career employee or the sum of three of the four-month summer hires.

They were a terrific bunch, those thirty-nine. During the summer, two guys with a garbage truck would leave Valdez on Monday morning and drive to Tok Junction. Along the way they would service all the parks at Keystone Canyon, Chitina, and all the other waysides, pick up the trash at all the rest sites, sell park permits, and give campfire talks. They'd pull out their sleeping bags wherever they stopped for the night. At Tok, they would turn around and work their way the 234 miles back to Valdez, servicing parks along the way. They would empty the garbage truck, take two days off, and start over. And they loved the work.

Mike Kennedy and Bill Hanable ran the historic preservation program with a tiny staff. They worked hard to keep the expanding construction boom from destroying valuable historic sites, and archaeologist Doug Reger did the same for the valuable evidence left by native people and the early non-natives. The route of early human migration from Asia passes right through areas considered for construction, and being watchdogs for these places was a serious job done by an understaffed group of professionals.

The State of Alaska was only fifteen years old when I was appointed. State Parks had evolved from a system of wayside camping areas managed by the Federal Bureau of Land Management. Other units had been added by the legislature from lands granted to Alaska at statehood. Neil Johansen, the chief planner, did the work of five people and later became the director of the agency. He put together the initial planning documents for some of the finest parks in the world and many of them have come to pass. Before the advent of oil money, the parks agency operated the largest state park system in the United States with the smallest staff.

There was almost no money available for improvements in what amounted to a rundown and often overused park system. In the summer, thousands of people used the parks on the Kenai Peninsula as bases for fishing when the king salmon runs returned. The primitive toilets overflowed and the fireplaces someone had formed out of cement and volcanic pumice would pop like little bunches of firecrackers and turn to rubble after a few campfires. In addition, the totem poles in Ketchikan were in need of maintenance, and the state budget was not available to fix any of this.

We proposed a bond issue for just over six million dollars and got it on the ballot for the next election. I traveled the state drumming up support, but the timing was poor. People were having huge arguments over the Native Claims Settlement Act and the expansion of national parks. Locals were often suspicious of parks eliminating hunting and some of the more destructive forms of recreation practiced on fragile lands. After listening to a couple of hours of complaining at a public hearing in Eagle River, I challenged the principal complainer, "You've told us what you don't want, now tell us what you *do* want." He replied, "In Eagle River we want to do anything we want to do, any time we want to do it, and in any damned place we want to do it." Meeting adjourned.

What happened in the election was fascinating. At midnight on election night, the bond vote was losing by about six hundred votes. We went home with long faces. But the votes from distant polling places hadn't come in yet due to winter weather and just the remoteness. Some voters were sixteen hundred miles from Anchorage and seven hundred or so from Russia. You could darn near throw a rock into Russian waters from Little Diomede Island, and getting the ballots in from that group of one hundred people and the twenty people who ran the light station on Attu are just two examples. Multiplying that by the number of other islands and remote snowed-in villages meant the final count wouldn't come until early January. It turned out that people who lived in places where no state park would exist voted for the bonds. During December, the gap kept closing and in the end we got the first adequate development money the parks had seen since statehood by a margin of less than one hundred votes. It was an Alaskan plurality.

Prize Fighting

The governor's chief of staff called and told me that some promoters wanted to stage a prize fight in Anchorage. The state had no bureaucratic department to deal with it and I was instructed that the promoters would call and make an appointment to obtain a permit. I was to become the boxing czar of the State of Alaska. I was also told that there was an "athletic commissioner," but that the position had been purely ceremonial in nature. "Who is it?" I asked. Sam Taguchi, it turned out, the owner of the City Café in Juneau. The reply took me aback.

It turned out that there were lots of prize fights held in events called "Smokers" in the territorial days. Governor and later Interior Secretary Wally Hickel had fought in them when he came to Alaska as an oilfield roustabout. Puggy Nelson, the foreman at Juneau Cold Storage, had been a fighter, and apparently Sam had as well.

I envisioned the worst possible outcome — suppose someone died in the ring. I'd be in court for the rest of my life. So I checked the statutes and they were of no help. I called a couple of friends in other states and cobbled together a permit that provided that a physician would be present and a few other provisions, had it typed up as an official document of the almost nonexistent Alaska Athletic Commission, and called Sam. Sam answered, and I envisioned him with his food-spattered towel wrapped around his waist. "Yeah?"

"Sam," I said. "Some guys want to have a prize fight in Anchorage. Is that okay with you?"

"Yeah," he replied and hung up the phone.

The permit was issued with the authorization of the athletic commissioner (telephone approval), I issued it to the promoters at a meeting in my office and locked my copies of the permits in my desk. The promoters offered me tickets but I didn't want to be anywhere nearby in the event of a disaster and I begged off because of a family commitment. The next morning I stopped for coffee on the way to work and checked the sports page of the morning paper and all had apparently turned out well. Now I could go back to running parks.

Wood Tikchik State Park

If there is a park where rangers go in an afterlife, it is this place. North of Bristol Bay, draining east from the Wood River Mountains, is a series of lakes between twenty and thirty miles in length plus one of fifty miles or so that bends around a place called Frog Mountain. The Wood River Lakes are connected by short river stretches and a kayaker or canoeist could spend a lifetime paddling there and never get to know it all. To the north, the Tikchik lakes drain east and south through the Nushagak system, meeting the Wood River near the town of Dillingham. The park is 1.6 million acres in size and is both the largest and the most remote wilderness state park in the United States. Runs of millions of sockeye salmon crowd their way up the river systems to spawn in the lakes, and four other species of salmon spawn there in lesser numbers. Trout, arctic char, and northern pike are abundant. Native people catch whitefish during winter and moose, caribou and Alaska brown bears are seen frequently and are hunted during certain hunting periods. While it seems strange that hunting takes place in this huge state park, there are no supermarkets in Aleknagik and the people who live around there have been good stewards of this place much longer than some of us latecomers.

During the winter of 1975–76, staff members and I traveled to Aleknagik Village and held a community meeting. The community wanted assurance that subsistence fishing and hunting would continue to be available to them in case the place was designated as a park. Everyone in the village came to the meeting and listened to our proposal and then they had us wait outside the school building while they discussed the proposal in the Yupik language. It was cold but we were dressed for it, and after an hour or so they invited us back in. The result was a good negotiation that led to the designation of a world-class park in 1978.

In the summer of 1976, Neil Johansen and his wife Betty accompanied Susie and me on a seaplane flight to the lakes. A Grumman Goose dropped us off on the north shore of Lake Kulik, where we assembled our Klepper folding kayaks. We spent a splendid few days paddling down the lakes and floating the class 1 and 2 rivers separating them. In the evening we would practice our bear avoidance techniques by fishing for our supper, cooking, cleaning up, and moving on to a campsite away from where we had eaten.

Neil and Betty were picked up by a float plane, and Susie and I continued on through lakes Beverly and Nerka. At River Bay, we were ashore poking through a willow thicket when we surprised a brown bear sow and two cubs. When the bear stood up to see what we were, I turned and said, "Don't run." By the time I had the words out of my mouth, Susie had a fifty-foot lead on me and I was running flat out trying to catch her. Running is supposed to trigger the predator's chase instincts and you are supposed to either stand your ground or walk quietly away. I have managed to do it on occasion, but when the adrenaline kicks in, it's almost impossible to remember that. We paddled the kayak off the beach and headed for deep water.

These days, there are fishing lodges and float planes that will take you anywhere they can land in the park, and there is now a permit system managed by the Alaska State Park System. My trip and the chance to work on saving this piece of pristine land from exploitation are highlights of my time working in Alaska state parks.

The Alaska Oil Pipeline was being built from Prudhoe Bay to Valdez and the state was about to become a North American version of an oil emirate. I spent a summer in Juneau working for Governor Hammond. In an office headed by future Lt. Governor Fran Ulmer, I worked on plans for what to do with the pipeline construction haul-road after the pipe was done. In effect, the pipeline construction had created a state highway across the 500 unspoiled miles from Fairbanks to Prudhoe Bay. The potential damage to the fragile arctic environment of unrestricted access to the highway was huge. During that period, I also helped develop an option for community grants, which would make some of the permanent fund oil revenues available for long-term improvements in Alaskan communities.

CHAPTER 24

Back To Big Basin

In September 1977 I got a telephone call from Huey Johnson, former head of the Trust for Public Lands. He had been appointed by Governor Jerry Brown to head up the Natural Resources Sector of California's state government. Huey asked me to become state parks director. This was full circle for me. I would be charged with administering and improving the parks I had grown up in. It was a huge leap for me, from managing a park system with thirty-nine people to heading up a system with thousands of employees and millions of annual visitors. The California State Park System was my dream job.

At the time, the state parks system had a backlog of more than $300 million in unspent bond funds and the state legislature was on the warpath. There was a railroad museum that had been in the making whose plans had been hijacked by hobbyists who were pushing for a huge warehouse in Sacramento to get all their rolling stock under cover, and the Symbionese Liberation Army had blown up the Summer House at Hearst Castle seemingly for the hell of it. Herb Rhodes, the first non-white California State Parks director, had just been reassigned to the Unemployment Insurance Board and minority employees of the parks system were fearing a return to what many considered an era of "white privilege." Whoever thought that government work is boring was wrong.

The deputy director was Alice Wright Cottingham (later Huffman). She was one of the more aggressive and able people I have worked with in a long career. I know we wouldn't have accomplished as much without her. She wrested back the control of the railroad museum and the other development projects and lit a fire under some of the people in the agency who needed it.

The museum planning was hired out to a firm that helped design the Smithsonian Air and Space Museum, and we ended up with a people-friendly unit instead of a warehouse. It has turned out to be a world-class museum. We finished the project on time and under budget. Concurrently, we managed the historic restoration of the state capitol building while it was undergoing an earthquake retrofit. We got a million-dollar appropriation and rebuilt and furnished the Summer House at Hearst Castle. The tours at Hearst actually make money for the state. It's the only unit that does.

Along the coast highway at Topanga State Beach in Southern California, the state had spent millions of dollars to buy the property separating the public from the beach. Several homes owned by state parks were leased to private citizens at low rates and some re-rented them at market rates for beachfront properties. Residents fenced off access and did everything they could to make the properties appear to be private property and not available to the public. I wanted to demolish the homes, but Governor Brown disagreed. He was aware of the critical housing situation in Los Angeles County and thought doing so didn't make sense.

A young Mexican-American man on my staff suggested a solution. A group known as Tijuana Express, probably named after Herb Alpert's band, would come north, dismantle the houses, salvaging what materials they could, and cart it all back to Mexico, where the recycled materials would be used in the construction of low-income housing. When I approached the governor and Huey Johnson with the scheme, they agreed, albeit reluctantly. A convoy of Mexican flat-bed trucks showed up and, instead of the usual bulldozer job, the workers carefully dismantled the houses and carried the materials south. The houses are gone and the beach is now open to all.

In another case, a group of Native Americans led by a man named Grandfather Semu and another fellow named Two Blue Jays came to my office and talked to me about the bones of Native Americans stored in a warehouse in West Sacramento. They wanted the bones returned. I went to the warehouse and found human skeletal remains stored in cardboard boxes on open shelves. The records were sloppy at best. Some bones had been dug up by homeowners who called the state, and the State Parks agency would collect them and store them for study. One record referred to the head of a Native American pickled in a large glass jar, but that item was nowhere to be found. I recalled stories of the severed head of the famous Gold Rush era bandit

Joaquin Murietta that had been displayed in saloons throughout California after his hanging and I wondered if that could be the missing head. I repatriated and turned over to Native tribes for burial several cardboard boxes of bones from a warehouse in West Sacramento—and was sued, unsuccessfully, by the state archaeology association. We never did find out what happened to the head.

Proposition 13, the first big cannon shot of the tax rebellion, was passed by the voters and Governor Brown ordered a 6% cut across the board. I talked him into exempting the state parks system from the cut if I could eliminate the operations management layer in Sacramento and open, on a primitive-use basis, sixteen parks that had been purchased but never opened. We reassigned more than a hundred people and managed to place all but two employees who couldn't move from Sacramento. The regional managers began to report directly to me.

The faces of California were changing. Minority groups were headed for majority status in many communities, and we ran a system of parks with very few representatives of those groups in uniform. Some progress was being made in the support staff area, but uniformed rangers were mostly "male and pale." I found many examples of park managers "swapping" with other managers to avoid being accused of nepotism. This common practice gave the children of current rangers a better chance at a permanent job. The practice was frowned upon, but disciplining the system would have been highly disruptive and time consuming. So I went to each person who was involved and told them if they were creative enough to do the swapping they would be able to figure out how to find a minority person for their next hire. They were on my list, and the way to get their name removed was to send me evidence of their compliance. That probably violated some personnel rules, but it worked, and the statute of bureaucratic limitations has probably run out by now.

One day Jane Matsuoka, my secretary, stuck her head in the door and told me that the actor Lorne Greene was on the phone and wanted to speak to me. The man who played Ben Cartwright on the *Bonanza* television show was on the line. We had recently lost a lawsuit over a land transaction we had with Mr. Greene along the coast of Los Angeles County. I answered and he got right to the point. He told me that he had no qualms about the lawsuit but that he loved state parks and wanted to make a gesture of reconciliation. He wanted to do one of our television spots without compensation. We agreed.

It was a hit. Back then, most public service announcements were aired at odd hours, but this one sometimes showed up on prime time. Lorne Greene's advertisement was followed by one donated by the singer Jose Feliciano, who talked about how a sight-impaired person could enjoy the parks. Our final spot had a great image boost for attracting minority employees. It featured Miss Black America in a park ranger uniform leading children on a nature walk. Afterward, we got many calls from rangers who wanted to know who she was and which park she worked in.

It wasn't always that peaceful. We got a tip that the Ku Klux Klan was planning an armed demonstration against immigration at Border Field State Park at the border south of San Diego. We had Alcohol Tobacco and Firearms agents join our rangers and stop the convoy at the entrance. Search warrants were served and there were several arrests. Later that summer, when I found out that the Klan planned to be armed during the operation of their recruitment booth at the state fair, I vetoed their application. Shortly after that, local Klansmen in Sacramento were arrested while making bombs intended for me and my family. When the Sacramento police raided the premises, they found papers pasted above the bomb assembly area on the kitchen table. On the papers entitled "How to Make Bombs" were the instructions. It appeared that these people weren't geniuses. For a week or so, police parked outside our home and accompanied my children to school, Susie to the store, and me to the office. We had police protection for a time.

A Notable Failure

William Penn Mott, one of the great people in the history of parks, was the executive director of the California State Parks Foundation. Bill had been the director of California's state parks and of the National Park Service. He was very successful with the foundation and managed to raise $15 million a year for projects in the state parks. Bill told me his biggest failure was in not convincing the legislature to authorize a state museum commemorating the motion picture industry. The Harold Lloyd estate was available to house collections, and a treasure trove of memorabilia had been offered by the actress Debbie Reynolds, who had been collecting it for years.

Even with offers of financial assistance from foundations, my pleas to the legislature fell on deaf ears. I was no more successful in that than Bill Mott. Not only that but during my tenure, Clarence Muse, one of the greatest of the pioneering African-American actors, a man who persevered during the most racist period in filmmaking, offered his extensive collection of materials commemorating the history of black people in the theater and films. There may be no more significant contribution to world culture from the United States than that of the motion picture. A museum on the order of one of the Smithsonian museums would have been a major draw to tourism and a place to gain an understanding of how films played such a role in the making of our culture. But it has not happened.

The Cahill Rule

With all of that interesting stuff, if you Google my name using my middle initial, what you get is the "Cahill Rule." Somewhere there is a law review article about that, but here's the story. A family with children showed up at my office wearing T-shirts that had their nude pictures printed on them. They handed me petitions signed by 40,000-plus registered voters asking for designated clothing-optional beaches. I took the petitions to the legislature and was told to have the State Parks Commission do it. The commission said, "*You* handle it." So, as the buck stopped in my office, hearings were scheduled in Sacramento, Los Angeles, and San Francisco. I assigned Richard Felty, our Southern California assistant director, to visit the sites that had been used by naturists for many years and to write a report. I was politically astute enough to delegate it to a guy who was a really good person but who was the opposite of flamboyant.

The hearings were, shall we say, entertaining. A stripper did her thing in front of the hearing in San Francisco and the press was all over it. The governor and the entertainer Linda Ronstadt were returning from a trip and when the governor got off the plane at Los Angeles International Airport, he was surrounded by the press who told him, "Russ Cahill wants to open the state parks to nudists." He simply said, "I think that's inappropriate."

Well, the next day I got the call, and the order was simply, "Fix it!" At the staff meeting, I asked for ideas, and an executive intern, an engineer from the Transportation Agency, said, "Let me have a go at it." The next day she came back with the plan that dealt with the issue without issuing new regulations. I issued an order to the rangers to not arrest except on the complaint of a visitor and only after the naked person refused an order to cover up the offending parts.

It worked for at least two decades but it was eventually challenged in court by opponents. My understanding is that the "rule" was found to be a non-rule by the courts because the hearings were not on the specific sites and a rule wasn't enacted through a more complex process. Anyway, people still take off their clothes at some remote beaches, but people who don't agree with public nudity still feel better about the whole deal, and there are occasional arrests.

CHAPTER 25

A Time of Sadness and Change

My tenure as director ended when my wife Susie's leukemia went downhill. I resigned, rented a little cottage in Cayucos, California, and acted as a nurse during her time. I believe the time was well spent. Susie outlived by two years the estimates made by her physician. At the end of a year, our resources had run out and it was time for me to get another job. I was interviewed by an executive search company that was recruiting for a job in Washington State. In 1981 Brian Boyle, newly elected commissioner of public lands, hired me to manage the Department of Natural Resources. A while after that, Susie passed away in Seattle after a tough battle.

During the ensuing thirty-three years I worked in forestry, fisheries, wildlife, and parks. I served as a visiting lecturer at the University of Washington for one year. For two years I directed the King County Parks and Natural Resources Agency and later managed The Washington Wildlife and Recreation Coalition, a startup non-governmental organization dedicated to funding parks, wildlife habitat, and disappearing agricultural lands.

One Final Job for the National Park Service

During the first year of the Clinton administration, in 1993, I was interviewed by Secretary of Interior Bruce Babbitt for the National Park Service director's job. Mr. Babbit was interested in my history of running the Alaska and California state park systems during the 1970s. The Secretary had interviewed Roger Kennedy, the director of the Smithsonian Museum of American History, for the job but invited me to also interview.

I traveled to the other Washington and spent some time in the US Senate and House of Representatives looking for support. Jolene Unsoeld, at the time the Member of Congress representing my district, was kind enough to set aside some temporary space in her office and I worked the phones and corridors looking for support. Senator Patty Murray had just been elected and I visited her in the temporary quarters in the basement of a Senate office building and she agreed to support me. Senator Slade Gorton's staff gave encouragement. I got support from Hawai'i senators Daniel Inouye and Spark Matsunaga, representatives Mink and Neil Abercrombie and the delegate from American Samoa, Eni Faleomavega. I got help from some of the Washington delegation and a few from California.

During my interview, Secretary Babbitt and I had a long discussion about Alaskan issues. Because of the Alaska lands legislation, passed at the end of the Carter administration, and the subsequent administration of millions of acres handed to Interior, the Secretary wanted to know what I'd do if given the opportunity. I was mindful of the job done by Theodore Roosevelt and Gifford Pinchot when they carved out the national forests during a lame-duck period at the end of TR's administration. I answered that I would work hard on the serious environmental protection issues and conclude as many of the negotiations as possible while the Democrats still had majorities in both houses of Congress because I believed the Republicans would gain a majority soon and that things would get tougher.

The following day, the Secretary appointed Roger Kennedy to head the agency. Roger and I had agreed to have lunch that day and during lunch he asked me to be his chief deputy. My wife, Narda Pierce, had just been appointed Washington State's first Solicitor General, and we had agreed that if I was appointed director, she would go with me to Washington DC. Anything less was not going to work for us.

I turned Roger down and he asked me if there were any jobs I could take to help him get started. Congress had recently agreed to decommission the Presidio of San Francisco as the Sixth US Army Headquarters and had authorized the National Park Service to take it over as a national park unit. I signed on for a six-month assignment as the director's representative and manager of the transition.

The Presidio of San Francisco

The Presidio of San Francisco is a national treasure. It was founded by the Spanish in July 1776 and the officers club is built around the remnants of the Alcalde, the residence of the traditional Spanish municipal magistrate, the oldest building in San Francisco. In addition, Civil War–era Fort Point sits under the south end of the Golden Gate Bridge. There are mule barns and stables where the black soldiers of the Ninth Cavalry kept their animals, and much of the earliest protection given to the national parks at Yosemite and Sequoia–Kings Canyon was done by the segregated units of the Ninth and the 24th Infantry Divisions. Of these men, 400, sometimes known as "Buffalo Soldiers," are buried in the national cemetery at the post.

Early experiments in military use of aircraft were done at Crissy Field, just inside the bay portion of the post. Wounded soldiers, sailors, and marines were treated at the Letterman General Hospital from its founding in 1898 during the Spanish–American War until it closed in 1994. At the end of World War II, more than 74,000 people were treated at Letterman. As headquarters for the Sixth Army, the Presidio saw many officers and enlisted soldiers quartered there, and many of our war dead of all services are buried there. Aside from all the historical value, this 1,491 acres of land may be the most valuable undeveloped land left within the city limits of any major city in the world, and lots of people had their eyes on it.

San Francisco, for all its colorful history, is a provincial place. Having been born and raised in and around the city gave me a leg up in dealing with the political aspects of the job. Nancy Pelosi, future US Speaker of the House, represented part of the district, as did Representative John Burton. Former San Francisco mayor Diane Feinstein and Representative Barbara Boxer both won election to the US Senate in 1993. All four of them wanted the project to succeed and helped at every step of the way.

During the contentious master plan hearings I chaired in that year, my friend Curt Smitch, the director of the Washington State Department of Wildlife, came to visit. In his time, Curt had been part of some of the nastiest public hearings I knew of, so he knew how bad it could be. He accompanied me to a hearing I was holding at Mission Street's El Centro de la Raza regarding the Presidio Master Plan, and he became curious about the odd goings-on. Attendees were incredibly kind and accommodating to aged or disabled people, and everyone helped set up Spanish language and American Sign Language interpretation at the hearing. People moved the chairs around so everyone could see and hear.

But once the hearing started, the gloves came off and proponents for everything from low-income housing to historic preservation argued on into the evening. After the meeting, when Curt asked about the dichotomy, I answered that San Franciscans stuck together on many social issues and on courtesy but were willing and able to fight it out on substantive issues. After the shouting subsides, I explained, everyone goes home in a reasonably civilized manner. At least that has been my experience.

For the time I was there, I had authority over a mixed group of people who were putting the complex plan for the future of the Presidio on paper. The planners, archeologists, historians, and others were scattered around in four different buildings, and my first action was to move them all into a Civil War–era barracks building and get them talking to one another. It turned out that not only had the work of putting together a complex master plan and environmental impact statement been largely completed, but the staff was eager to get on with it, and only the fear of political problems somewhere up the ladder had been causing everyone to move slowly on the whole thing.

Having no future in the Park Service ahead of me turned out to be a great advantage. We edited the documents, got illustrations and maps put together, held hearings, and published the two huge documents. While the plan has had a lot of tweaking done by Congress and others, the Presidio is turning out to be one of the crown jewels of our country.

Roger Kennedy went on to be an innovative parks director, and Don Neubacher, one of the people most responsible for the Presidio plan's success, has become superintendent of Yosemite National Park. I returned to Olympia and worked for Washington's state parks until my retirement.

CHAPTER 26

Author's Note

Time is marching off with my memories, but there appear to be a few hours left on my parking meter on this planet. So before I disappear from the scene, I thought I'd plunk down a few memories. I recognize that some of what I write may be what's left after memory filters out all the bad stuff but if you remember this differently, I have some advice; write your own book and we'll have an argument over a beer.

Horace Albright

The training center at Grand Canyon is named for Horace M. Albright, the first employee and the second director of the National Park Service. Horace grew up in the Owens Valley of Eastern California, where his father was involved on the losing side of the water wars between land owners and the City of Los Angeles. A graduate of the University of California and Georgetown Law School, he served as the superintendent of Yellowstone National Park and later, as director, was responsible for the additions of the

Great Smoky Mountains, Grand Teton, and other significant parks.

Over the years I got to know Horace and spent time with him. On a long ride to see one of his projects, the Pacific Botanical Gardens property in Hawai'i, Horace, then in his eighties, shared a couple of anecdotes with me. It seems that when he took over as superintendent at Yellowstone, park employees had formed a chapter of the Ku Klux Klan and were holding evening meetings in the park. Horace told me he had to force them to go outside the park for their meetings. I had heard rumors of Klan activity in the parks, but this was directly from the Horace's mouth.

He also related a funny story about the maintenance worker in Yellowstone who solved a problem in an innovative way. In the 1920s most men and boys carried pocket knives. When spending time in the park outhouses, many of them whiled away the time carving graffiti in the walls. One of the workers solved the problem by putting powerful springs on the doors and removing the locks. Seated vandals had to hold the inward swinging door closed with one hand while doing their business and were unable to coordinate the action with their artwork. Years later when the workers would meet one another, they would laugh, crouch, and hold one arm forward palm facing out in a greeting known only to them.

The last time I saw Horace was in Washington, DC. He was raising hell with the American Institute of Architects (AIA) for their plan to build a modern building adjacent to the Octagon Building, their national headquarters. Horace told me the Octagon Building was one of the only original buildings left from early days in the city and he considered the plan an abomination. He was well into his 80s and still keeping a watchful eye on the nation's treasures. The AIA went ahead and built it anyway, but Horace gave them a good fight.

What Was Your Favorite Park?

I get asked this frequently. The parks I was assigned to are all A-list parks. My answer is always the same. The park I worked in was my favorite park. It's easy for me to say this, but I mean it sincerely; I love every one of the county, state, and national parks I have worked with. My friend, the historian Bill Brown, wrote a book about park management called *Islands of Hope*. Ever since I read it I have thought of these places, both big and small, in the image of Bill's title.

You have read my take on the places I've worked, but I'm going to tell you of seven places in the West you might not have visited. These are places I love. There are places like this throughout the US and Canada as well as other countries. Check them out and then make your own list.

Ranald Mac Donald's Grave

Let's begin with the tiniest state park in Washington. Ten miles from Curlew, just south of the US–Canada border, situated above the Kettle River is a Native American graveyard. Buried there is Ranald Mac Donald, the son of a Chinook woman and one of the principals of the Hudson's Bay Co. Mr. Mac Donald was a whaler, a miner in Australia, and one of the first western visitors to Japan. He rowed a small boat ashore onto Japanese soil in 1848, some years before the country was officially open to the West, and was captured and tried by the officials in Nagasaki who forbade the landing of foreigners. While spending seven months in Japan, he taught English to several Japanese, including one who interpreted during the visit of Commodore Matthew Perry. Mac Donald is held in high esteem by many in Japan, and Japanese visitors to the US rent cars in Seattle and drive to Ferry County to pay respects. I have found Japanese coins left on Ranald's grave. The park is unremarkable, but the trip across the mountains, the setting of the place, and the story of this largely forgotten American make it worth the trip. Take your lunch.

A Place to Take a Walk

One of my first jobs in Washington State was to supervise the purchase of the Milwaukee Railroad right of way from Idaho to the watershed just east of Seattle. After the task was completed, Narda and I decided to walk the whole route. In June 1990 we put on our backpacks, caught a ride to Tekoa at the Idaho border and walked the John Wayne Pioneer trail across our state. The western half of the trail is listed as the Iron Horse State Park. While the trail is 253 miles long, there were another fifty or so miles needed to walk on streets and roads to our destination, the Pioneer Dock in Seattle.

If you visit this trail you can walk one mile or hundreds of miles and there are places to park and camp along the trail. In winter you can ski the trail from snow parks in the Cascade Mountains, and it has been a great place to take children for their first cross-country skiing. On our walking trip we saw both white-tailed and black-tailed deer, coyotes, and a couple of badgers. Young owls peered at us from burrows along the abandoned road cuts and avocets were wading around in Crab Creek west of Othello, Washington. The walk up along the Yakima River toward Snoqualmie Pass is spectacular. Go for an afternoon or do what we did and take a month.

Theodore Roosevelt's Ranch

From an overlook high above the Little Missouri River as it curves east to its meeting with the main river, Narda and I once watched a herd of a hundred or so bison come out of the forest and cross the river. It was as if we were transported back in time to a place where perhaps a Hidatsa hunter watched a similar scene and prepared himself to bring home meat and hides. Today, it is part of the North Unit of Theodore Roosevelt National Park. It is one of the more remote parks in the coterminous forty-eight states, but it draws me back time and again. I admit that as a child I was addicted to the early western movies with their ignorant and racist depictions of native peoples coupled with fantastic scenes of the big-sky west. Working in or visiting these parks gives you the same views without the stupid dialogue.

Where Dinosaurs Walked

Now we head south to Glen Rose Texas, a little south and west of the Dallas–Fort Worth metropolitan area. In the Brazos River and in the rock formations nearby are the tracks of dinosaurs. The mud traversed by these creatures eventually turned to rock, and you can follow the tracks around the area both in and out of the river. This is Dinosaur Valley State Park. If you have children who know dinosaurs only from their iPhones or cartoon representations, you should take them to this park. The creatures of the *Jurassic Park* movies were here and you can feel down inside the footprints and discover the nature of those long, sharp claws.

Down River

The Brazos River meanders across Texas and passes another state park. This one near Houston is worth a look. If you are a birder, or just an amazed onlooker, the Brazos Bend State Park is a great place to spend an afternoon or an overnight. Brilliant spoonbills and other birds not found up north are abundant. There are alligators and turtles and all sorts of other creatures. While riding bicycles through the park we had to stop and let two copperhead snakes cross the road in front of us. After that, walking to the park restroom in the campground after dark didn't appeal to us. By the way, the Texas state park system has posted one of the more informative warnings I have seen. As I recall, it reads, "If you own a dog, don't throw sticks in the water for the dog to retrieve. The alligators consider the dogs lunch." The best deal is to climb the observation tower with binoculars and enjoy some of the best nature viewing around.

A Little Different State Park

If you head west on Interstate 10 from Houston you will pass through Las Cruces and come to Deming, New Mexico. South and east of there, in the mountains, is one of the more remarkable state parks in the country. For the price of admission to New Mexico's Rockhound State Park, you can have a nice hike and excavate rock specimens up to about a bucketload and take them home with you. I have spent a career asking people not to remove rocks from parks and would often use the old saw, "Just think what this place would look like if everyone took a rock home." Well, the answer here is, it would look just about the same. The rangers have a reference collection laid out so you can compare your specimens, and there is camping, but it's pretty full during high season. Take your bucket and rock hammer and have at it.

Into the Desert

If you continue west you will find yourself in California. South of I-10 and stretching almost to the Mexican border is Anza-Borrego Desert State Park. This 600,000-acre park is home to more than 250 borregos, or desert bighorn sheep. The park goes from sea-level playas up to 6,000-foot peaks and the sea-level portions are just uphill from the Salton Sea, which is 230 feet below sea level. The sediments in this park have disgorged fossils of animals of all kinds and are still doing so. Check out the "underground" visitor center to learn about the fossil evidence and hike the trail to a native palm oasis a couple of miles up from the campground. You may be dive-bombed by hummingbirds in some seasons. One great thing to do in this park is to camp out off one of the dirt roads. Unlike most parks, you are allowed, with some sensible limitations, to camp in the wilds. Sleeping in the open in a sleeping bag under a dark sky is an experience we don't get with all the electric lights around cities.

The World's Oldest Profession
Visits the Parks

If you visit Skagway and the Klondike-Gold Rush National Historical Park, you will see some of the photographs of women who followed the Gold Rush, intending to provide certain services to lonesome miners. There is even a tour of one of the former brothels. Creek Street in Ketchikan is another place where this part of the history of the wild and woolly days of old are interpreted. In modern times, rangers told me that places called "hot pillow establishments," where rooms were rented by the hour by prostitutes, operated in the Lake Mead National Recreation Area until the Park Service shut them down.

The modern version of these pleasure palaces followed the oil pipeline workers to Alaska during the 1970s. On an otherwise uneventful day in late spring, I received a call from the crew who were assigned to open the campground at Keystone Canyon State Park east of Valdez. When the two summer employees got to the campground, it had already been opened and they reported that there were two large recreational vehicles parked in the campground with queues of off-duty pipeline workers lined up waiting their turn to partake in whatever recreation was going on inside. "What should we do?" one of the summer employees asked me. "Don't try to break it up," I said. "See if you can talk to whoever's in charge."

When the employee called me back, he reported that the woman running the operation had tasked their "off-duty" employees with cleaning up the campground, purchased state parks annual permits for all of their vehicles, and was going to move on before the park employees made their weekly return trip back from Tok. I assumed that the operation found other places to invite their customers near the construction camps, and we didn't hear any more from them.

Trinkets

Somewhere among the mess of souvenirs clustered in niches around my house is a bear; as bears go, this one is really not much. Perhaps four inches is the maximum height this bear will ever achieve. Under the bear's chin a thermometer is embedded in his or her belly and its name is engraved just at its feet. The bear's name is, "A Souvenir of Yellowstone National Park." I don't recall which Asian country this bear originated in, and I assume its parent was carved by some artisan and then reproduced by the thousands.

Some of my collection of paintings and prints are worth more money; none are valued any higher. One of my nephews, on a trip to Yellowstone, thought of me and bought the bear as a gift. I appreciate his choice. He could have purchased a fake totem pole made in Korea or a plastic gorilla. These things and a hundred thousand others show up in the national park concessioner shops all over the country.

Of course, they are not the only choices. In Yosemite Valley, you can visit the late Ansel Adams's shop and spend four or five figures on original prints made by the great man's own eye and hands. In Glacier Bay National Park there are original works by Native American artists that are stunning and stunningly priced. Part of the story of the history of Hubble Trading Post National Historic Site near Ganado, Arizona, is that it's still a trading post and Native American artisans bring their blankets and rugs and have them displayed for sale. I don't think my nephew considered purchasing those trinkets when he spent his lawn-mowing money on my bear.

Keeping the arts and crafts of America alive is part of the mission of the National Park Service. It is an appropriate role. Foreign-made or even non Native American–made trinkets are not appropriate at Hubble. Navaho rugs sold by the artisans at the South Rim of the Grand Canyon shouldn't be competing with lower-priced rugs made elsewhere. But somewhere there ought to be a place for people to buy small remembrances of their trip to the Grand Canyon.

There are people in the National Park Service who consider themselves purists. They don't believe there should be sales of Asian or south of the border–made trinkets in the parks. If that becomes the case, my young relatives will not be coming home with the little talismans we carry with us in our houses and the memories these things invoke.

When I was the superintendent at Haleakala National Park, *Vogue* magazine requested permission to film some of their models down in the crater. "It's not appropriate," came back the argument from staff. "Why not?" I asked. It turned out there wasn't any good argument. So a couple of months later we were treated to the sight of several very slender women and their photographers riding horseback in a pack string headed down the Halemau'u cliffside trail headed for the ranger cabin at Paliku.

The results of the trip were varied. The reluctant ranger I assigned to keep the tenderfeet safe and out of trouble grumbled about it; the models had extremely sore rear ends due to their lack of natural padding, and the photographs featured in an edition of the magazine were spectacular. One showed a model who was either perspiring greatly or had been rubbed down with oil, supposedly using a rope to pull herself up a sliding red sand area near the center of the crater. The action of the model was a little absurd, but the stunning outfit shown against the backdrop of the colorful volcanic background was worth it all. Tens of thousands of people who would not ordinarily be exposed to the beauty of their national park got to enjoy it.

Safety in Bear Country

I am not an expert in bear attacks. The experiences I have shared with you are a small sample of incidents regarding bears. During the last century, North American bears have killed about three people per year. Many victims were killed over the carcasses of elk, moose, or deer they shot while hunting. Some were killed by zoo or captive bears and on some occasions drunks fell into zoo enclosures and were killed. Several were infants or young children taken from the outside of cabins or yards in bear country. More than one victim was getting close to take photographs of the bear that ended up killing him. And some people, a remarkably small number, were just the unlucky ones who were hunted down by our biggest North American land predator. Black bears made most of the kills but are much more abundant than grizzly bears. To make a comparison, each year dogs kill about twenty-seven people and lightning ninety. That is not comforting to those who hike, camp, and live in bear country, but it puts the issue in perspective for those of us who love to be out in the wilds.

My advice to those who ask about bear safety is always the same. Listen to the lectures and warning briefings in the parks. One fellow killed in Yellowstone refused the briefing, saying he was a "bear expert." *Read and heed warning postings.* Be observant and make noise while hiking in bear country; surprising a grizzly is not a good idea. Secure food and garbage and never feed a bear either inadvertently or on purpose. A predatory bear may look at your sandwich as an appetizer and you as the main course. But most of all, learn about the bears and their habits. Some of what I know about bears is from my experiences over the years, but the best guidance for me is from a book entitled *Bear Attacks Their Causes and Avoidance* by Stephen Herrero. If you spend time living, working, or recreating in bear country it is a mandatory read.

Advice to a New Park Ranger

Love your park and show that love in your interaction with visitors. I admit it; I was lucky. The parks I was assigned are all on the prime list for rangers. But I could have gone to Pinnacles National Monument or Colonial National Historical Park or any of hundreds of interesting places in this country. I compared the possibilities of some small relatively unknown park with the alternative of working for the Civil Service

Commission and it was no contest. I have visited a lot of these places and know I'd have been able to enjoy working there too. Dream about your favorite park but love the park you're with.

Don't ignore your companions. If you are married, have children, or have a companion, make sure you work hard to make their life complete. It can be a lonely existence in many remote parks and the people who accompany us need to have a life as well. Often our companions are as well or better educated than we are. Many are talented artists and musicians. Work hard to help with their choices.

Get the hell out of the office. Look at the place through a visitor's eyes and learn something. Notice changes in patterns of nature and the people who come to see it all. Talk a little and listen a lot. Photograph the exhibits and compare them annually to see if they are faded or vandalized and get them replaced.

Try everything. If you are an enforcement ranger, volunteer to conduct interpretive walks and evening programs in the event of illness or absence. You will need to know a lot more about your park than just where the speeders are or what time the bar at the lodge gets rowdy. Read everything you can about your park, including criticism. If you are a naturalist, volunteer for fire duty and rescue work. Historians should spend a weekend doing trail or landscape work. Earn a first-aid instructor's card and teach people in and around the park.

Find some old timers in the community and record their memories about your park. Write it up in a newsletter or blog post. If your park doesn't have one, start one. If your park is located in a place with a substantial minority population, get to know people and encourage adults and children to visit and to consider a career in parks. The country is changing and the Park Service, by its nature, is a conservative entity, slow to change. Be an agent of that change.

Don't join the group of park employees who dislikes their patrons. I know; the person who stops his car in the middle of the road in front of you, and discharges a family of five into the roadway with cameras with no regard of anyone else, looks like an idiot. He or she isn't. They may just be on vacation from a really boring job and their brain is on vacation as well. Courteously herd them back into their car and direct them to an overlook.

Don't give verbal warnings to dangerous drivers. If you pull someone over for seriously excessive speed or reckless driving on the ancient roads we have in many of our parks, write them a ticket. And don't lecture them. The ticket is the lecture. Be pleasant but firm and you won't spend all your off days in the magistrate's court.

I have watched contemporary enforcement rangers take very aggressive postures when approaching visitors, sometimes even in non-enforcement situations. Body language alone can escalate relatively harmless situations into confrontations that no one can back down from. My friend Paul Malmberg, a retired state ranger, recommended to his employees a process called verbal judo, which is a common sense method of getting the job done with fewer unnecessary arrests. There are ways to remain protective of your own safety while not appearing to be ready for an octagon fight. Think of the hours of paperwork this avoids.

Cultivate relationships with local law enforcement. You may need each other when things get really nasty, and for heaven's sake, be careful out there.

October 2015, Highway 41: Wawona to Chinquapin

I am driving up to the valley to spend some time doing research for this book. My rental car is locked into one of those classic national park auto serpentine convoys. The Toyota Prius in the lead is going well under the 35 MPH speed limit and the serpentine is getting longer. The speed limit is a little slow, but with thirty Yosemite bears dead from auto strikes this year, it's not unreasonable.

All of a sudden the whole convoy goes into one of those herky-jerky compression modes as the Prius slows and some device akin to a frog's extensible tongue comes out the passenger side window. In an incredible act of tourist-narcissism a woman is taking a selfie at 20 miles per hour.

I'm practicing a lack of self-control by shouting obscenities inside my rental car. It doesn't do any good, but finally the whole caterpillar-like convoy starts going again and I pull off, extract a lined pad from my satchel and write for a while.

After the Wawona Tunnel I see a big column of smoke coming up from the south side of the valley. Along the road are a dozen or so fire vehicles and crews setting fires. A large preventive burn has been ignited for three miles or so along the south side. I stop and talk to a firefighter who is controlling traffic. His name turns out to be Jim Tucker, and his dad Tom was a former colleague of mine from the 1970s. Jim tells me they've been planning to do this for forty years and the weather and park management are finally in concert so the burning is happening.

One thing this tells me is that the superintendent, Don Neubacher, doesn't mind pulling the trigger on planned actions. That hasn't always been the case. The huge Yosemite Rim Fire of 2013 burned a quarter of a million acres of national forest and park land. One of its causative factors was the amount of woody material left from suppressing fire over the years. This preventive burn will take away much of the burnable litter, keep the big trees alive, and allow their seeds to reach the soil and reproduce. You may see some charred stuff when you visit the valley, but you'll be looking at a healthy ecosystem. Times have changed in the last 50 years.

Gustavus 2015

On the back cover of *Hope and Hard Work* by James Mackovjak, there is a quote: "It's o.k. to get mad at people, because that's normal. But living out here in the tules you couldn't stay mad at them, because then you wouldn't have anybody to play pinochle with." — Ruth Matson. Ruth was a schoolteacher back in the 1930s who came to teach a half-dozen children in a little schoolhouse. Over the years she wrote delightful columns from Gustavus and sent them to the *Juneau Empire* newspaper. Her husband Fred was a fisherman. Today, Aimee Youmans's guest house sits on the old Matson homestead.

Down the road a bit from Amy's guest house there is a small Saturday market outside the Sunnyside Store where people sell local crafts, a few veggies, and locally made cosmetics. On a sunny day in July, I unfolded the Cabela's chair that Narda bought for me out on the lawn next to some local folks who sold metal art, jewelry, vegetables, and baked goods. I sold and signed more than a dozen copies of my novel, *Kolea*. The chair is equipped with what I'd call a foldout beer table and the store sells lattes and hot soup and sandwiches, so I was having a pretty good afternoon shooting the bull with all the aging hippies and other friends I have known for going on five decades.

It happens that there is a writers' group in Gustavus. I think my novel is at least the 20th book published by the authors of this tiny town. People get together once a week for coffee and read and criticize each other's work. The attendees vary from a seventeen-year-old young woman who writes very good poetry to septuagenarians like me who have written novels, memoirs, and other works.

There are also music groups. The library bought a bunch of ukuleles and people gather for strumming on a weekly basis. And there is a music night at the library. You have probably not experienced music played by guitars, both acoustic and electric, mandolins, saxophones, flutes, violins, and whatever anyone else plays, executed by folks with varied amounts of skill, all at the same time. When solo time comes around, a mandolin-accompanied English folk song, performed by a matronly lady, may be followed by some hard licks on an electric guitar pumped out by an under-20 guy. Somebody usually has some kind of drum.

The music stuff reminds me of the odd phenomenon one finds in remote places. In the bush, people of really varied backgrounds share recreation and other social happenings. The national epidemic of divisiveness has changed that for the worse, but when we had a forest fire in this area a few years ago, people who get their politics from Rush Limbaugh and Fox News were shoulder to shoulder with vegans and those who get their politics from *Mother Jones*.

There is a friend of mine who is very conservative. I am a liberal. If I have a heart attack, I expect she, a volunteer EMT on the fire department, would be the person most likely to keep me alive. I am certain I would do the same. Looking at the current national political silliness, I think about the bumper sticker I once saw. It said, "Less Barking, More Wagging." Maybe we could have, "Less Shouting, More Strumming."

This would seem an odd place for a Hawai'ian to return to every year. But we Hawai'ians are people of the sea driven by a desire to wander. Perhaps there is also a longing for a more simple existence in my mixed-up DNA. In Hawai'i we gathered lots of our food from the surrounding forest and sea. The same happens here in this remote place. And there are no condominiums. What started in Big Basin has ended up here.

—Russell Cahill, 2016

ACKNOWLEDGMENTS

I owe many people for help with the writing of this memoir. I thank you all. Special thanks to: Yosemite Research Librarian Virginia Sanchez; the staff of the Lacey, Washington, branch of the Timberland Library; Chuck Janda of Port Angeles, WA; Cleve Pinnix and Paul Malmberg of Olympia, WA; Don Neubacher, superintendent, Yosemite National Park; Doyle Fanning for help with photos; Elizabeth Flynn for edits and formatting and Gwen Gades for cover design, and the rest of my posse, Julia Goldstein and Jeanne Freed.

About the author

Russell Cahill lives in Olympia, Washington, with his wife, Narda Pierce. Russell joined the National Park Service in 1966, fifty years after its founding. He served at Yosemite, Glacier Bay, Katmai, and Haleakala National Parks and was assigned for a year to the President's Council on Environmental Quality in Washington, DC. He has been the director of parks in King County, Washington, the states of Alaska and California, and a manager in Washington State Parks. Russell's career in natural resources spans forty-eight of the last fifty years. He is the author of *Kolea*, a story about ancient Hawai'i.

Information about Russell Cahill and his books may be found at russellcahill.com.

BIBLIOGRAPHY

Albright, Horace M. [1985]. *The Birth of the National Park Service: The Founding Years, 1913–33,* Howe Brothers, Salt Lake City, UT. As told to Robert Cahn.

Bohn, Dave [1967]. *Glacier Bay: the Land and the Silence,* Sierra Club: San Francisco.

Brown , William E. [1971]. *Islands of Hope,* National Recreation and Park Association.

Cahill, Russell [2016]. *Kolea,* Dragon Moon Press.

Cobb, Hubbard [1950]. *Your Dream Home and How to Build It for Less Than $3,500,* Wm. H. Wise & Co.

Daws, Gavan [1973]. *Holy Man,* University of Hawai'i Press.

Herrero, Stephen [2002]. *Bear Attacks: Their Causes and Avoidance* (revised edition), Lyons Press.

Ise, John [1961]. *Our National Park Policy: A Critical History,* John Hopkins Press.

Mackovjak, James [1988]. *Hope and Hard Work: The Early Settlers in Gustavus, Alaska,* Goose Cove Press.

Matson, Ruth O. [1972]. *Happy Alaskans, We,* Goose Cove Press.

Wenkham, Robert. *Maui: The Last Hawaiian Place: From the Earth's Wild Places,* A Friends of the Earth Series.

Made in the USA
San Bernardino, CA
04 October 2016